Contents

Foreword by Lord Hutton of Furness

As we have all come to appreciate in recent years – whether we work in the private or public sectors – providing good quality pensions is becoming a much more challenging task given the increasing length of time that most people can now look forward to spending in retirement. This is particularly true of defined benefit pensions, where a pension is ultimately determined by the level of a person's earnings, rather than the level of their pension contributions. Defined benefit pensions make up most of the pensions on offer to public service employees and they raise substantial issues of affordability as well as risk sharing. As my interim report makes clear, there have been important attempts made to address the underlying drivers that have seen costs of providing public service pensions increase sharply in recent years. I welcome these reforms as they have helped to strike a better balance between employees and taxpayers in the distribution of pension costs. But as my report also makes clear we must satisfy ourselves that we have fully and openly addressed all of the underlying pressures that are still pushing up the cost of providing public service pensions. To do this properly we need to expose all the real costs of providing the current range of public service pensions as well as understand the real benefits they represent to employees.

The public sector performs functions that are vital to the security of our country, the success of our economy and the health of our society. There is therefore a compelling public policy objective in being able to recruit and retain the best possible people for these crucially important jobs. As many people have rightly pointed out in their evidence to me, we should regard public service pensions as part of an effectively designed overall remuneration system that will allow us to achieve this end. In doing so we need to keep firmly in mind the need for fairness and efficiency in the use of scarce public resources. And whilst it is right that taxpayers finance a proportion of public service pensions, as they are also the recipients of the services that are provided by employees, they are also entitled to expect that their hard earned money is spent wisely and to the best possible effect right across the public sector.

First and foremost, pensions are provided in order to ensure an adequate income when someone stops working which can help them sustain a reasonable standard of living without becoming a burden on the welfare state. If we lose sight of this when we consider the case for reform and end up pushing more people into a reliance on state benefits in retirement, we may well find that overall costs are likely to rise, whatever changes might be made to the design of public service pensions. Simple, sloganistic approaches are not the answer. Any reforms must try and avoid this obvious pitfall.

My interim report therefore attempts to establish a proper baseline from which we can answer the fundamental question – are public service pensions on a fair and sustainable footing that provides the best possible value for money to the taxpayer as well as adequate retirement incomes for public service employees? It is my clear view that the figures in this report make it plain that the status quo is not tenable. I believe we need to adopt a more prudent approach to meeting the cost of public service pensions in order to strike a fairer balance not just between current taxpayers and public service employees but also between current and future generations. In the short term, however, I consider there is also a strong case for looking at some increase in pension contributions for public service employees, to better meet the real costs of providing these pensions, the value of which has risen in recent years with most of these extra costs falling to taxpayers. Ministers should, however, proceed carefully and ensure adequate protection and proper safeguards to protect accrued rights, avoid undue hardship and minimise the risk of any rise in the number of employees who opt out of scheme membership. In particular, I would not recommend introducing contribution rates for the armed forces at this time. This issue should be dealt with in a way that is consistent with any long-term reforms.

In undertaking this review, I have been struck both by the enormous complexity of the subject matter, as well as by the degree of misunderstandings and confusions that surround any debate about it. My report tries to dispel some of these myths. It is mistaken to talk about 'gold-plated' pensions as being the norm across the public sector. In the most part, the pensions that are paid out to public service employees when they retire are fairly modest by any standard, although in part these reflect part-career or part-time working. For some people these modest pensions now look over generous because of the changes that have taken place in the private sector over the last 30 years or so, where pensions have become generally much less valuable than they used to be. Fewer people in the private sector are also contributing to a pension. I hope these negative trends can be reversed and I fully support efforts to do so.

This downward drift in pension provision in the private sector does not however provide sufficient support or justification in my view for the argument that pensions in the public sector must therefore automatically follow the same course. I regard this as a counsel of despair. In making clear I believe there is a case for further reform I have therefore rejected a race to the bottom as the only answer, and hope that reformed public service pensions can be seen as once again providing a benchmark for the private sector to aim towards.

My final report will therefore look at a wider range of radical solutions that might represent a better balance between the need for fairness between taxpayers and scheme members – allowing for increasing longevity – and the need to ensure adequate retirement incomes for those who have devoted some or all of their careers in the service of the wider community. It is for this reason and to ensure that public service pension schemes represent the best possible value for money to the taxpayer, that I have set out a set of general principles that should guide and govern the appraisal of all of the options for longer-term reform. Each of these options will be assessed against these general principles. I consider that the public sector should continue to set a good standard as an employer and this includes a good standard of pension provision that seeks to avoid widespread opt-out of public service employees from these pension schemes. Promoting a responsible approach that encourages employees in the public sector to save for their retirement should be uppermost in our minds.

My interim report has also tried to tell the full story of who benefits most from the current system. Final salary schemes, which are the norm across much of the public sector, primarily reward high earners who progress rapidly through the salary scales. I am concerned that this may no longer provide a robust and fair mechanism for the majority of the public service workforce. I will return to this issue in my final report.

Pensions are long-term commitments and any reform I propose must protect the rights that public service workers have already accrued. The recommendations in my final report will ensure these rights are protected and I am taking advice on how this might best be defined. However I am clear that protecting accrued rights does not extend as far as protecting current terms for future pension accrual.

Finally, I have looked at the issue of how we currently deal with the pensions of those employees who move from the public sector when services are taken over by new providers. It would be unwise to allow the current arrangements to apply an unintended brake on the development of a more mixed economy of providers in the public sector. There is, at present, a danger of this happening. This issue will be dealt with in my final report and will form part of my appraisal of long-term reform options.

My final report will be completed next year. I am extremely grateful to all those who have submitted evidence to my Commission to date and to the panel of experts who are advising me in this work. I intend to conduct the widest possible consultation over the next few months as I now begin to examine options for long-term structural reform. I hope to build the widest possible measure of consensus about the way forward. I realise this will not be easy. But it is my belief that in finalising my recommendations, it will be possible to design a set of solutions that meet and address the principles I have set out in this interim report.

Lord Hutton of Furness

Executive Summary

The importance of public service pensions

Ex.1 Public service pensions provide retirement incomes for millions of people in the UK. In total there are 12 million active, deferred or pensioner members and dependants of public service pension schemes. That is around one in five people in the UK. Each year schemes pay out billions of pounds to their pensioners – in 2008-09 payments were £32bn, about two-thirds of the cost of the basic State Pension.

Ex.2 Many of the current public service pension design features, including accrual rates, pension ages and the link to final salary, date back nearly 200 years, despite the enormous upheavals in demography and in the nature of work in our economy. In 1841, someone who reached the age of 60 might expect to live a further 14 years on average, but most people did not live to this age. By the early 1970s, when the schemes were substantially reformed, the life expectancy of a 60 year old had increased to about 18 years and this has now risen to around 28 years. In addition, many more people can now expect to reach 60.

Ex.3 In the past the public service pension schemes have provided a lead for employers in the private sector, but more recently there has been significant divergence. The pensions landscape in the private sector has been varied, but over the first two thirds of the last century the number of people in private sector pension schemes grew, almost all of which followed the defined benefit structure of the public sector. Over the last third of the century and the start of this century, the picture has been very different.

Ex.4 The general trend from the 1950s has been one of increasing public service provision – particularly once allowance is made for the inclusion of many nationalised industry scheme members within the public sector figures for the 1950s to the 1980s. This is set against a fall in provision in the private sector, especially in defined benefit provision, which is not fully offset by the increase in defined contribution provision.

Ex.5 The trend is increasing, with a sharp fall in defined benefit provision in the private sector since the late 1990s. Whilst the provision of defined contribution schemes has increased significantly, there are still a growing number of employees with no provision. In fact, around 85 per cent of public sector employees have some form of employer sponsored pension provision compared to around 35 per cent in the private sector.

Chart Ex.1: Private sector employees by type of pension provision

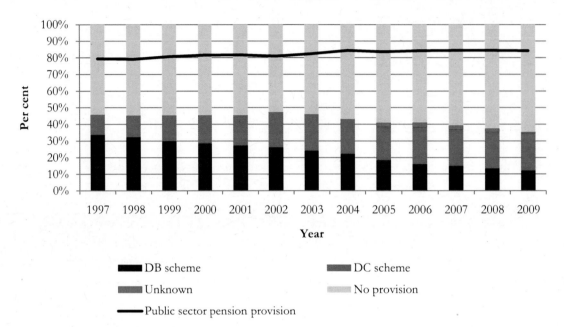

Source: *Annual Survey of Hours and Earnings, 2009*

Ex.6 This divergence between the public and private sectors is of concern, particularly in the context of mobility between the public and private sectors. However, it does not necessarily follow that public service pension schemes should be modelled in future on what has been happening in the private sector in recent years, especially given the decline in private pension provision and the concern that saving levels in the private sector are not currently optimal. It is important to take into account other issues as we consider future options, including the need to ensure public service pensions provide adequate retirement incomes for retirees.

Ex.7 The key question regarding public service pensions is whether they fit the needs of a modern flexible workforce, whilst being affordable, sustainable, adequate and fair to both taxpayers and employees.

The need for reform

Ex.8 The need to modernise public service pensions has been recognised for some time, in particular the need to deal with increasing costs: between 1999-2000 and 2009-10 the amount of benefits paid from the five largest public service pension schemes increased by 32 per cent.[1] This increase in costs was mainly driven by an increase in the number of pensioners, a result of the expansion of the public service workforce over the last four decades, longer life expectancy and the extension of pension rights for early leavers and women.

---

1 Based on estimates by the GAD undertaken for the IPSPC. IPSPC analysis of schemes Resource Accounts.

Ex.9 The previous Government recognised these issues and in 1997 started a series of significant reforms. These included:

- limited increases in pension age for groups such as the uniformed services, mostly for new entrants. In the civil service, NHS and teachers schemes existing members were allowed to keep a pension age of 60 if they wished, but new entrants have a pension age of 65 and pension ages lower than 65 will be phased out by 2020 in the Local Government Pension Scheme;

- sharing of risk arising from demographic change in the form of 'cap and share' rules. This spreads the cost of any future unexpected increases in contributions more equitably between employer and employees than previously, up to a cap after which any future increases would be borne by the members. Cap and share at present applies to the four biggest schemes – NHS, teachers, local government and civil service, although it has not yet affected employee contributions in any scheme and the Local Government Pensions Scheme does not yet have a cap set; and

- changed accrual rates for many of the reformed schemes, particularly for new entrants, but all except the civil service are still based on final salary. The change to a career average structure in the civil service scheme was not primarily undertaken as a cost saving measure, but as a response to the changing nature of the workforce.

Ex.10 More recently the current Government changed the measure of annual price movements, so that from April 2011 onwards pensions uprating will move from the Retail Price Index (RPI) to the Consumer Price Index (CPI).

Ex.11 This change in the indexation measure may have reduced the value of benefits to scheme members by around 15 per cent on average. When this change is combined with other reforms to date across the major schemes the value to current members of reformed schemes with CPI indexation is, on average, around 25 per cent less than the pre-reform schemes with RPI indexation.

Ex.12 All these past reforms, the current pay freeze and planned workforce reductions will reduce the future cost of pensions. The gross cost of paying unfunded public service pensions is expected to fall from 1.9 per cent of GDP in 2010-11 to 1.4 per cent of GDP by 2060 as the central projection of Chart 1.B shows.

Ex.13 However, these measures will take many decades to fully affect the costs of pensions in payment, which are heavily influenced by existing pensioners, the vast majority of whom are still in pre-reform schemes. The Commission estimates that gross expenditure on unfunded public service pensions will remain close to current levels as a proportion of GDP over the next decade.

Chart Ex.2: Projected pension payments as a percentage of GDP – sensitivity analysis

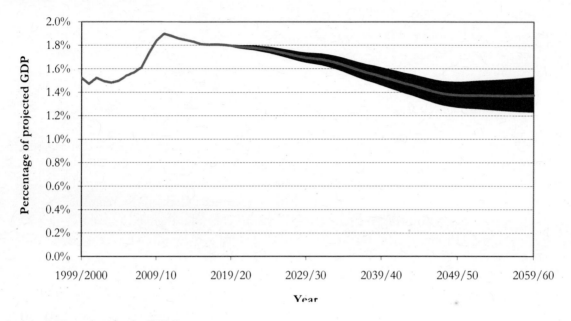

Source: GAD analysis for the IPSPC

Ex.14 As Chart 1.B also shows, these costs are inherently uncertain and sensitive to assumptions on life expectancy, size of workforce, earnings growth and the implementation of planned reforms. How long pensioners will live has been systematically underestimated in the past, as Chart 1.C below shows. These issues could impact on the sustainability of these schemes in the future.

Chart Ex.3: Actual and projected period life expectancy at birth for UK males

Source IPSPC analysis drawing on C Shaw 2007 and ONS 2008 population projections.

Ex.15 The expected proportion of adult life spent in retirement has increased as people live longer. A male pensioner in the NHS scheme who retired at 60 today is expected to spend 41 per cent of their adult life in retirement compared to 28 per cent if they retired in 1955. This means the value of a public service pension in 2003-04 is expected to be around a third higher than it would have been if assumptions about life expectancy were the same as those in 1955.

Ex.16 The increase in longevity also means that these pensions are now likely to be paid out for longer, increasing the overall costs. These extra costs, despite recent reforms, have not been equally split between employer and employees. Although the way costs are divided varies from scheme to scheme, the significant majority is met by the employer and by extension the taxpayer, as the Chart 1.D shows. This is not unique to public service pension schemes, but when many of the public service pension schemes were introduced employers and employees paid similar levels of contributions to the scheme – now employers pay around twice what employees contribute in most of the schemes and sometimes more.

Chart Ex.4: Employee contributions as a proportion of the overall cost of accrual (pre and post reform)

Source: IPSPC and PPI

Note: Figures based on effective employee benefit rates described in Box 5.B.

Ex.17 In addition, there is also uncertainty over whether the total contributions paid reflect the costs of the benefits received. The current discount rate used to set the level of total contributions in schemes was set in the late 1990s. Initial work by the Commission suggests that the current discount rate is at the high end of what is appropriate. The Commission is asking the Government to review this rate, ideally so that the findings can inform the final report.

Ex.18 In assessing fairness the Commission also found that the reliance on final salary in the majority of public service pension schemes tends to favour those who receive rapid promotion and those who stay in public service for their whole career. The promotion effect alone could mean that high flyers can receive almost twice as much in pension payments per pound of employee contributions than do low flyers.[2]

Ex.19 In addition, there is an issue of fairness between different pension schemes. This is particularly true between pre and post reform schemes given the protections given to most existing members when the schemes were reformed.

Ex.20 Public service pensions need to be considered in the context of the total benefits package for employees. There is no evidence that pay is lower for public service workers to

---

2 'Should Defined Benefit Pension Schemes be Career Average or Final Salary', Sutcliffe, C., ICMA Centre Discussion Papers in Finance, DP 2007-6, 2007.

reflect higher levels of pension provision. Consequently current pension schemes do not appear to offer best value for money.

Ex.21 Evidence to the Commission has also made it clear that current pension structures, combined with the requirement to provide comparable pensions ('Fair Deal'), are a barrier to non-public service providers, potentially reducing the efficiencies and innovation in public service delivery that could be achieved.

Ex.22 It has been suggested that extending access to public service pension schemes for non public service employees could be a solution to this problem. But it is not clear that this provides a solution either for the Government, which has to accept additional liabilities and long-term risk, or for some external organisations, which, depending on the scheme they are entering, may be required to pay a premium or indemnity for entry, take part in deficit recovery plans, or pay large exit charges.

Ex.23 When examining transparency it was clear that the debate around public service pensions has been hampered by a lack of consensus on what are the key facts and figures and a lack of transparency of the relevant data. This report seeks to provide as comprehensive a picture as possible in order to supply the basis for well-informed debate. In the final report the Commission will consider ways in which transparency and scrutiny can be improved.

Ex.24 The Commission has also come to the conclusion that it remains reasonable to continue to operate arrangements without actual funds as the basic financing model, given the risks, lack of obvious economic benefit and transition costs of moving to a fully funded model. Equally, there is no reason to de-fund existing funded schemes.

The principles of public service pension provision

Ex.25 This is therefore an appropriate time to take overall stock of the situation and begin to address the underlying issues of scheme design and management of costs into the future. The Commission has identified a set of principles against which long-term options for reform should be judged. These are:

- *affordability and sustainability* – what level of pension cost is affordable is a political decision for the Government within the context of a range of priorities. But it is not an issue that can just be looked at in the short-term. In assessing affordability and sustainability we have identified a range of relevant cost measures to consider and the need for an agreed discount rate. Part of any assessment of cost must include the consequences of any reform on increased take-up of benefits such as pension credit. Critical to sustainability is the sensitivity of future costs to risks, such as changes to longevity and how these risks are managed as well as shared;

- *adequacy and fairness* – public service pensions should provide an adequate level of retirement income for public service workers with a reasonable degree of certainty. To assess reforms against this principle we need an agreed measure of what is adequate and what should be measured against the benchmark. We provide some ideas in this interim report. Adequacy is a measure of fairness, but we are also looking at fairness in the distribution of contributions and benefits between members of the same pension scheme; fairness between different schemes; fairness between generations of taxpayers; and fairness between the taxpayer and the public service employee;

- *supporting productivity* – to support productivity, public service pension scheme design should be consistent with an efficient labour market for employees. This should allow the taxpayer to be confident that public services are being delivered on a value for money basis. In general, scheme design should avoid barriers to the movement of employees between sectors. This needs to be viewed in the context of the whole remuneration package and whether the schemes support the recruitment and retention of the right people in the right jobs in a cost-effective way and deal flexibly with specific job issues. In particular, they should not be an unintended barrier to the outsourcing and mutualisation of public services that could drive greater productivity and efficiency in public services; and

- *transparency and simplicity* – public service pensions should be widely understood, both by the scheme members with regard to their own specific entitlements and possible future benefits; and by taxpayers who have a role in funding the schemes. The key design features and the costs to employers and employees need to be set out clearly and transparently. Assessment of reform needs to consider potential trade-offs together with implementation and transitional issues, including the means for protecting accrued rights and possibilities for more cost-effective administration. It is also important that public service pension schemes, like schemes in the private sector, have a clear legal framework and have effective and accountable governance structures.

Options for change

Short-term options

Ex.26 The issues around fairness, sustainability, promoting productivity and the need for transparency and simplicity mean there is a need to consider long-term structural reform of public service pensions. However, that reform will take time. Increased longevity, the imbalance between employer and employee contributions and the fact that total contributions may be too low if the discount rate is too high suggests there is a case to make short-term changes, pending long-term reform.

Ex.27 The Commission considered a range of options that may provide short-term savings, specifically:

- changing the benefits structure;

- contracting public service pension schemes into the State Second Pension; and

- increasing contribution rates.

Ex.28 Of these, the most effective way to make short-term savings is to increase member contributions and there is also a clear rationale for doing so.

Ex.29 It is a matter for the Government to decide the manner and level of any increases in contributions necessary. However, the Commission feels that any increases should be managed so as to protect the low paid and, if possible, increases in contributions should be staged and need to be considered with a view to preventing a significant increase in opt out rates. The Commission does not recommend introducing contribution rates for the armed forces at this time.

Long-term options

Ex.30 The current public service pensions structure was not designed for modern working patterns and has been unable to respond flexibly to changes in this area and to demographic change over the past few decades. This has led to:

- rising benefits due to increasing longevity;

- unequal treatment of members within the same profession;

- unfair sharing of costs between the employee, the employer and taxpayers; and

- not realising the potential for plurality in the ways public services are provided.

Ex.31 Long-term structural reform is needed, as these issues cannot be dealt with through traditional final salary defined benefit schemes. But neither can they be dealt with appropriately through a funded, individual account, defined contribution model for all employees, which would place a major financing burden on taxpayers, ignore the ability of Government as a large employer to manage certain types of risk and increase uncertainty of post-retirement income for scheme members, which is difficult in particular for the low paid to manage.

Ex.32 In the Commission's final report a range of alternative structures will be considered. This will include a career average alternative to the current final salary defined benefit schemes. Drawing upon international experiences, alternatives such as Sweden's use of notional defined contribution schemes and the Netherlands' collective defined contribution schemes will be examined, as will risk sharing models, such as hybrid schemes that combine elements of defined benefit and defined contribution models. The Commission will also consider elements of scheme design, such as, ensuring normal pension ages are in line with the latest developments in longevity. This will enable the Commission to make a recommendation on a range of options to the Government, which can establish a more appropriate framework for public service pensions going forward.

The Landscape

Independent
Public Service
Pensions Commission

1 The pensions landscape

Box 1.A: Summary

- Many features of public service pension schemes are a historical legacy, including accrual rates, pension ages and final salary structures.

- Most public service pension schemes are unfunded, defined benefit (DB) final salary schemes. Normal pension ages are usually 60 or 65, but some are lower, particularly for uniformed services such as the police. There is significant variation in the percentages of pay that employees contribute to their schemes.

- While public service pension schemes once led the way in terms of scheme features, they have not kept pace with changes such as improvements in longevity. They have also not been developed in a fully coherent way, with a multiplicity of complex provisions and overlapping coverage of various categories of public servants and employers.

- Around one in five UK citizens has some entitlement to a public service pension. The total amounts paid out are large: £32 billion in 2008-09, about two thirds of the cost of the basic State Pension.

- There is considerable variation between payments to public service pensioners. The average (mean) amount of pension paid is around £7,800 per year (falling to £6,500 when the payment of pensions to dependants is included) and about half of pensioner members receive less than £5,600 per year. 90 per cent of pensioner members receive less than £17,000 per year.

- State pensions have undergone significant reform in recent years. Changes to the basic State Pension and the State Second Pension will increase the numbers who receive State pensions and the amounts paid to lower earners. There are also planned increases in the State Pension Age to deal with increasing longevity. A review of whether the timetable for these increases should be advanced was announced at Budget 2010 in June.

- Meanwhile in the last few decades pension provision in the private sector has increasingly diverged from the public service model, in response to pressures around longevity, changes in the business environment and investment risk. This has led to a sharp decrease in the provision of DB schemes and an increase in the number of employees without any provision at all. Governments, past and present, have therefore attempted to address the inadequate level of pensions coverage in the private sector.[a] The move towards automatic enrolment of employees into occupational pension schemes is an important step forward in tackling this problem.

a The new Government's 'programme for government' says that We will simplify the rules and regulations relating to pensions to help reinvigorate occupational pensions, encouraging companies to offer high quality pensions to all employees, and we will work with business and the industry to support auto enrolment (page 26).

Public service pensions history

1.1 Public service pensions are more widely available, have longer histories and have been subject to less structural change than their counterparts in the private sector. The principal features of public service pensions have remained largely unchanged since their introduction even though the original reasoning may no longer fully apply.

1.2 Some features, such as pension ages of 60, final salary structures and accrual rates, go back to civil service terms of the 19th and early 20th centuries, or even earlier – the civil service scheme being the original public service scheme.[1] The earlier pension ages enjoyed by most members of the police, firefighters and armed forces schemes also date back to the 19th and early 20th centuries.

1.3 At that time life expectancy was much lower than today. In 1841, someone who reached the age of 60 might expect to live a further 14 years on average, but most people did not live to this age. By the early 1970s, when the schemes were substantially reformed, the life expectancy of a 60 year old had increased to about 18 years and this has now risen to around 28 years. In addition, many more people can now expect to reach 60. Life expectancies for members of public service pension schemes are typically assumed to be higher than these national average figures (see Chart 4.D).

1.4 This increase in longevity represents an increase of about a third in the cost of providing a pension since the mid 1950s.[2] For public service employees, most of the cost of this increase has so far been met by employers and therefore taxpayers.

1.5 The link between pension and final salary is also long-standing, with its roots in the 17th century. Although the formulae used have changed over time, they have always been based on earnings in the last few years before retirement.

1.6 The accrual rate of 1/60th of final salary for each year's service dates from the civil service scheme in 1859 and the accrual rate of 1/80th of final salary, plus 3/80ths for a separate lump sum, was introduced for the civil service in 1909.

1.7 The employee contribution rates – the percentage of salary that employees pay as an explicit contribution towards pension costs – have changed somewhat in recent years, but the general levels still reflect the historic legacy. For example, the civil service scheme only had standard contributions for members from 1972, initially only to pay for dependants' benefits. It retains rates of 1.5 per cent or 3.5 per cent. Employee rates of 5 per cent or 6 per cent for teachers, local government and the NHS date back to the first half of the 20th century. The average rates today are around 6.5 per cent.

1.8 There has not been a standard formula for determining the proportion of cost to be covered through employee contributions. However, some of the initial contribution rates,

---

1 An explanation of the key terms used in this report can be found in the glossary at Annex G.
2 Chapter 4, paragraph 4.42

such as for teachers and local government, were designed so that employees would meet half of the costs.[3] At other times, such as when police and firefighters employee contributions were revised in the 1980s, the intention was that employee contributions should cover one third of the cost.[4]

1.9 Historically public service pensions have led the way in design features. For example, they gave men and women the same pension ages long before other schemes and pioneered inflation protection (in 1920), pensions for leavers before retirement age and transfers of rights between schemes.

1.10 However, it is fair to say that the development of public service pension schemes has not been a planned and fully coherent process, and there is a plethora of complex provisions. Different schemes, designs and contributions apply to people employed in similar public service jobs, sometimes for the same employer. For instance, school teachers in England and Wales are usually members of the Teachers' Pension Scheme, while teaching assistants are usually members of the Local Government Pension Scheme (LGPS).

The public service pensions landscape

1.11 Public service pension schemes range in size from the LGPS, which in total have well over 4.5 million members, to arrangements set up for one or two individuals. Total payments to public service pensioners and their dependants were almost £32 billion in 2008-09; lump sums account for a fifth of these payments. This compares to £50 billion paid through the basic State Pension[5] so the importance of public service pensions to retirement incomes is evident.

1.12 In total, about 12 million people are members of a public service pension scheme, or receive pensions as dependants of deceased members.[6] So about one in five UK citizens has some entitlement to a public service pension. There are around three hundred public service pension schemes, but more than 95 per cent are members of the six largest categories of scheme – local government, NHS, teachers, civil service, armed forces and police.

1.13 Most of the schemes have common features. Almost all provide DB pensions.[7] Employer contributions are substantial in all schemes. All are based on final salaries except

---

3 Under the Local Government and Other Officers' Superannuation Act 1922 and the Teachers (Superannuation) Act 1925. The Local Government Superannuation Act 1937 and the Teachers (Superannuation) Act 1956 provided for employers to make supplementary contributions if the standard employer and employee contributions were insufficient to meet costs identified at valuations.

4 That change and the corresponding change in employer contributions from half to two thirds, seems to reflect the increasing regularity and value of post-award pensions indexation during the second half of the 20th century and the point that the arrangements for providing that indexation in the unfunded schemes at first left such costs only with the Exchequer.

5 Department for Work and Pensions Resource Accounts 2008-09.

6 Pension schemes' Resource Accounts, 2008-09.

7 The main exception is the civil service 'Partnership' defined contribution option for those who joined since 2002.

the latest ('Nuvos') sections of the civil service schemes, which are based on career average salary and the general and dental practitioner sections of the NHS schemes (which are based on career average earnings or profits). Annex B summarises the key features of the main public service pension schemes.

1.14 There are also important differences between public service pension schemes. Normal Pension Ages are usually 60 or 65, but they are typically lower in the police and armed forces. There is substantial variation in the proportion of pay that employees contribute to their scheme, ranging from zero in the armed forces to 11 per cent of pay in the pre-2006 police and firefighters schemes. The operation of public service pension schemes is described in Box 1.B.

Box 1.B: The operation of DB public service pension schemes

Some public service pension schemes, such as the Local Government Pension Scheme and the Medical Research Council Pension Scheme, are funded, as are UK private sector pension schemes. Employers and employees pay their contributions into a fund and these contributions are invested in assets that produce investment returns. Current pensions are paid from the fund. Funds can be in surplus or in deficit, depending on for instance, investment returns and the development of liabilities. If investment returns are lower than expected, contribution rates might increase to reduce any deficit, but, because these are DB schemes, low (or high) investment returns should not affect pension payments.

Most public service pension schemes are unfunded, or pay-as-you-go, including those for the NHS, teachers, the civil service and the uniformed services. In an unfunded scheme, current pension contributions, both from employees and employers, are treated as revenue. In practice these contributions are used to help offset the cost of paying pensions to current pensioners. But contribution rates are usually calculated so that the contributions received should reflect the future cost of the pensions for current active members when they come into payment. Current contributions therefore have no direct relationship to the amount of pensions currently in payment.

This means that current contributions from employers and employees may exceed, or fall below, the amount of pension benefits currently in payment, depending on factors such as the size of the current workforce compared to those receiving pensions. For example, receipts from employee and employer contributions to the NHS scheme in England and Wales (totalling £8.1billion in 2009-10) currently outweigh the cost of paying pensions and lump sums (£6.1 billion in 2009-10). In contrast, contributions to the armed forces scheme totalled £1.7 billion, compared to pension and lump sum payments of £3.5 billion.[a]

a NHS and AFPS Resource Accounts 2009-10.

Box 1.B (continued): The operation of DB public service pension schemes

The diagram below shows the flow of money in the four largest unfunded schemes in 2009-10. Contributions from employers (£13.1 billion) and employees (£4.6 billion) in respect of current employees have been used to cover much of the cash costs of pension payments (£20.8 billion). The gap of £3.1 billion is treated as if it was met by balancing payments from the Exchequer, ultimately from general government taxation.[a] The funding of pension schemes is discussed further in Chapter 4.

Diagram: Payments and contributions in pay-as-you-go pension schemes

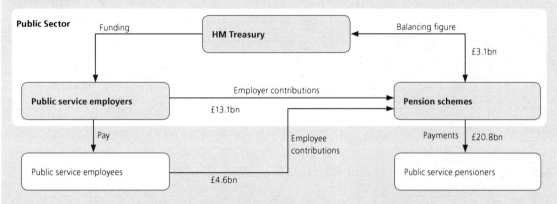

Source: The cost of public service pensions, National Audit Office. Figures from Resource Accounts 2009-10.

Note: The payments figure includes lump sum payments as well as pensions. For National Accounts purposes (which are separate from the Treasury's public spending treatment), the ONS treats employer pension contributions as part of pay and thus outside the public sector boundary.

a In practice the amounts needed to meet the gap are provided scheme-by-scheme, through departments' requests to Parliament for resources.

Scheme membership

1.15 As set out in the Commission's terms of reference,[8] the review covers public service pension schemes, including those for civil servants, the armed forces, NHS employees, teachers, local government employees, the police, firefighters, the judiciary and the research councils. There are also several smaller schemes that are not specifically part of the review but which will be required to act on its recommendations. The review does not cover pension schemes in the wider public sector, such as those for the BBC, the Bank of England and the Royal Mail. These schemes are administered by trustees, rather than being authorised by statute and the organisation concerned sets the scheme's rules. Nor does the review cover the pension fund for Members of Parliament, although the Government has stated

---

8 See Annex A.

that it believes that decisions about the parliamentary scheme should be informed by the Commission's final recommendations.[9]

1.16 The review looks at public service pension schemes across the UK. The devolved administrations have slightly different arrangements for administering public service pensions. For instance, Scottish Ministers have the power to make secondary legislation affecting how the five Scottish public service pension schemes operate (including, for example, the benefits the schemes provide and contributions made by scheme members). In practice the schemes have tended to mirror each other closely and they face similar structural issues.

1.17 The two largest categories of scheme are those for local government and health workers, with over seven and a half million members between them (Chart 1.A). The proportions of active, deferred and pensioner members differ significantly between schemes. The NHS schemes have relatively large numbers of active members, reflecting recent expansion of the workforce, while the armed forces scheme has relatively more pensioner and deferred members due to the young age at which most members leave and the reduction in the size of the armed forces since the 1950s.

1.18 There are over three million deferred scheme members, with particularly high numbers in the armed forces and relatively few in the police and fire services, where most members continue until retirement. Differences here are likely to reflect different career structures and the degree of role specialisation.

Chart 1.A: Scheme membership in UK pension schemes

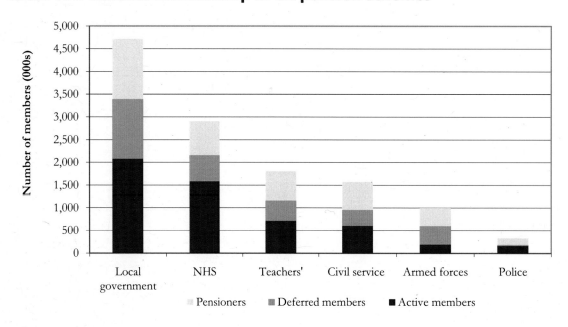

Source: IPSPC analysis of resource accounts and scheme data returns

Note: Police data and local government data in England and Wales are from 2008-09, all others 2009-10.

---

9 Hansard, 26 July 2010.

Age

1.19 The age distribution of scheme members varies according to historic changes in employment levels and staffing needs. For instance, more than half of active members in the armed forces scheme are below thirty years old. The age structure of the NHS scheme is shown in Chart 1.B. There is a large spike of active members in their forties – almost half a million of the 1.4 million working members of the scheme. Most members in their sixties have retired, reflecting a normal pension age of 60 for most members in the pre-reform NHS scheme.[10] More than half of pensioner members are below 70 years old.

Chart 1.B: NHS scheme membership by age

Source: Data returns from NHS England & Wales and NHS Scotland

Earnings

1.20 Of the schemes for which the Commission has data, just over three quarters of active members have pensionable earnings between £15,000 and £40,000 per annum – four per cent earn less than this, while 18 per cent earn more (see Chart 1.C). There are around twice as many female active members as male and median male earnings are about ten per cent higher than female earnings (between £30,000 and £33,000 per annum compared to between £27,000 and £30,000). Just over one per cent of active members earn more than £100,000 per annum, most of them members of the NHS scheme.

---

10 Some nurses and Mental Health Officers still have a normal pension age of 55.

Chart 1.C: Earnings of active members

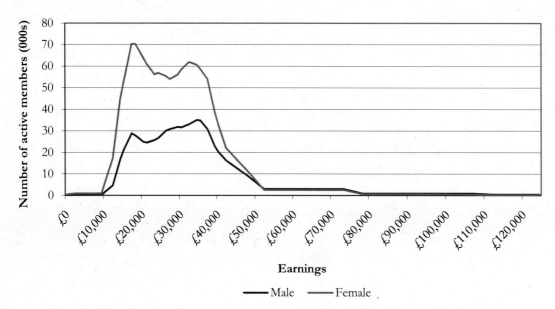

Source: IPSPC analysis of scheme data returns.

Note: Schemes covered are NHS (England & Wales), police (England & Wales) (as at 31 March 2008), teachers (all of UK), armed forces, principal civil service (UK and Northern Ireland), judiciary. A moving average is used to smooth the raw data.

Membership over time

1.21 Pension schemes are not static, but instead change as public services and the UK's population change. The number of pensioners in the five largest schemes[11] has increased by 27 per cent in a decade: almost 700,000 additional pensioners (Table 1.A). This is due to several factors, including the expansion of the public service workforce over the last four decades, longer life expectancy and the extension of pension rights for early leavers and women.

---

11 The NHS and Teachers' Pension Schemes in England and Wales, the Principal Civil Service Pension Scheme (UK), the Armed Forces Pension Scheme and the Local Government Pension Scheme in England.

Table 1.A: Pensions in payment over the last decade

	Number of pensions in payment		
	At March 2000	At March 2010	% change
Local government (England)	859,000	1,088,000[a]	27
NHS (England and Wales)	450,900	638,610	42
Civil service (UK)	528,500	592,000	12
Teachers (England and Wales)	415,984	567,012	36
Armed forces	335,306	398,840	19
Total	2,589,690	3,284,462	27

Source: The Cost of Public Service Pensions, National Audit Office, IPSPC analysis of resource accounts and Local Government Financial Statistics England, 2010.

a Local government membership is from March 2009.

1.22 The number of active scheme members has also risen, particularly due to expansion of the NHS, teaching, and local government. In the late 1960s, there were fewer than 400,000 active members of the NHS pension scheme, little more than a quarter of the current level.[12]

Pensions in payment

1.23 The increase in the number of pensioners has been the main factor in increasing total pension payments in the last decade. Excluding lump sum payments, pension payments to pensioners and dependants from the five largest schemes were over £21 billion in 2009-10 (see Table 1.B). The average pension payment has increased slightly in real terms since 1999-2000, but the increase in the number of pensions in payment has resulted in a 32 per cent real-terms rise in total payments during the decade.

1.24 Care must be taken in interpreting these numbers. They include pensions of those who have worked part time or have only worked in the public sector for a small proportion of their career. The Commission does not have detailed data to adjust for these effects. Also, the figures here include pensions paid both to pensioner members and to their dependants. Since dependant pensions are typically lower, the mean pension here (£6,500) is lower than the mean pension paid to members only (which is about £7,800 across all schemes).

---

12 The Complete Guide to Pensions and Superannuation, Gilling-Smith, 1968 and IPSPC data request.

Table 1.B: The evolution of pension payments from the five largest schemes

	Total Pensions Paid			Average (Mean) Pension		
	1999-2000 (adjusted to 2009-10 prices) (£bn)	2009-10 (£bn)	% change	1999-2000 (adjusted to 2009-10 prices) (£)	2009-10 (£)	% change
Local government (England)	3.53	4.41	25	4,115	4,052	-2
NHS (England and Wales)	3.13	4.62	47	6,951	7,234	4
Civil service (UK)	2.97	3.67	23	5,626	6,199	10
Teachers (England and Wales)	4.07	5.56	37	9,781	9,806	0
Armed forces	2.40	3.08	28	7,160	7,722	8
Total	16.11	21.34	32	6,222	6,497	4

Source: The Cost of Public Service Pensions, National Audit Office, IPSPC analysis of resource accounts, Local Government Financial Statistics England, 2010.

Note: Average pensions are calculated by dividing total pensions paid in the year by the number of pensions in payment at the end of the year. This typically overstates average pensions by about one per cent. Local government figures are for 2008-09, indexed by RPI inflation to 2009-10.

1.25 Chart 1.D shows the percentage of pensions paid to pensioner members that are below a particular level, as well as the proportion of total payments to pensioners that are at that level or lower. For example this chart shows that that about 65 per cent of female pensioners and 40 per cent of male pensioners, receive pensions below £6,000 per annum. Though these constitute more than half of pensioners, the pensions make up about 16 per cent of total payments. About 1 in 10 male pensioners and 1 in 50 female pensioners, receive pensions of more than £20,000 per annum. Pensions of this size or larger constitute about 25 per cent of the total amount of pension payments paid out, though they are received by only about five per cent of pensioners.

1.26 Male public service pensioners typically receive more than female pensioners – the median male pensioner receives just over £8,000 per annum, while the median female pensioner receives just under £4,000 per annum. This gap can be explained in part by a combination of more fragmented female careers (particularly connected to caring responsibilities), differential rates of part-time employment (there are currently more than seven times as many female part-time public service workers as male ones)[13] and historic differences in careers and consequently in pensionable pay. The fairness of different pension scheme designs is discussed in Chapter 5.

Chart 1.D: Cumulative distribution of pension payments and pensioner members

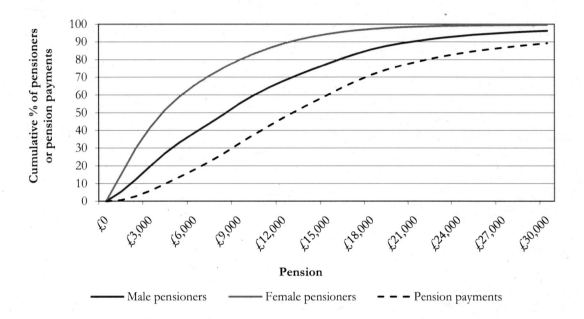

Source: IPSPC analysis of scheme data returns.

Note: Scheme categories covered are local government (England & Wales and Northern Ireland), NHS (UK), teachers (UK), civil service (UK and Northern Ireland), armed forces, judiciary, police (England & Wales), fire (England) and research councils (UK). The local government scheme in England and Wales is based on pensions in payment in 2007, while the police scheme is based on pensions in payment at 1 April 2008.

Variability between and within schemes

1.27 Pension payments vary considerably both within and between schemes. Almost half of LGPS recipients receive less than £3,000 a year, while more than half of police pensioners receive at least £15,000 a year. Police pension payments are fairly tightly clustered around the average (mean) of £15,650, but NHS payments are very dispersed. Three quarters receive less than £9,000 a year, but one per cent receives about £55,000 or more. Differences in average pension levels reflect different earnings paths and work patterns between the categories of scheme.

1.28 Table 1.C looks at the top and bottom of the pension distribution in more depth. One in ten public service pensions are £1,000 a year or less. More than half of these small pensions are from local government work, while most of the remainder are from the civil

---

13 For example, in 2007 there were 443,000 female part-time workers in the English local government scheme compared to 42,000 male part-timers.

service and NHS schemes. Pensions at this level will typically be the result of both short service and relatively low pay, perhaps because of part-time work.

1.29 The top ten per cent of pensioners receive at least £17,000 per annum. These are fairly evenly distributed between schemes, though the police and fire services are over-represented (more than a third of police pensioners are in this top ten per cent) and local government is under-represented (four per cent of local government pensions are at this level).

1.30 The top one per cent, receiving at least £37,000 per annum, is dominated by the NHS, which represents almost two thirds of the pensions paid at this level or above – mostly long-serving doctors. The NHS continues to be strongly represented in the top 0.1 per cent and top 0.01 per cent of the distribution. About one in six judicial pensioners receives over £67,000 per annum, placing them in the top 0.1 per cent of the distribution of public service pensions.

Table 1.C: The distribution of pension payments 2009-10

	Total pensioner members	Mean pension payment	Median pension payment	Pensioners receiving per annum			
				At most £1,000	At least £17,000	At least £37,000	At least £67,000
				Approximate position in distribution			
				Bottom 10%	Top 10%	Top 1%	Top 0.1%
Local government	906,184 (29% of all pensioner members)	£4,777	£3,048	179,533 (58%)	35,441 (12%)	2,704 (8%)	104 (4%)
NHS	673,029 (22%)	£7,510	£4,087	77,712 (25%)	65,154 (21%)	21,351 (62%)	2,328 (79%)
Teachers	580,046 (19%)	£10,858	£10,275	9,309 (3%)	81,632 (27%)	2,845 (8%)	73 (2%)
Civil service	483,536 (16%)	£7,632	£5,023	38,530 (12%)	51,000 (17%)	3,515 (10%)	166 (6%)
Armed forces	305,695 (10%)	£8,834	£7,987	3,851 (1%)	26,231 (9%)	1,981 (6%)	70 (2%)
Police	104,044 (3%)	£15,636	£15,583	741 (<1%)	38,077 (12%)	645 (2%)	33 (1%)
Fire	28,959 (1%)	£13,804	£13,193	239 (<1%)	6,479 (2%)	288 (1%)	* (<1%)
Research councils	10,128 (<1%)	£9,110	£6,254	1,012 (<1%)	1,876 (1%)	49 (<1%)	0
Judiciary	1,061 (<1%)	£53,876	£52,565	0	1,037 (<1%)	874 (3%)	178 (6%)
All schemes	3,092,682 (100%)	£7,841	£5,603	310,927 (100%)	306,927 (100%)	34,252 (100%)	2,960 (approx.) (100%)

Source: IPSPC analysis of scheme data returns

Note: * indicates that there are between 1 and 10 pensioners here. Scheme coverage is the same as that in Chart 1.D. Local government data in England and Wales are from pensions in payment in 2007, while police data are from pensions in payment on 1 April 2008. This table looks at pensioner members only, not including dependants, so figures differ from those in Tables 1.A and 1.B. The median is calculated through linear interpolation of the available data. For instance, the median payment from all public service pension schemes is between £5,000 and £6,000. If pension payments were distributed uniformly in this band, the median would be £5,603, as stated.

1.31 One important reason for differences in pension payments is length of service. Chart 1.E shows that this is a key determinant of the distribution of pensions from the UK's teachers' pension schemes.

Chart 1.E: Pensions in payment from UK teachers' pension schemes

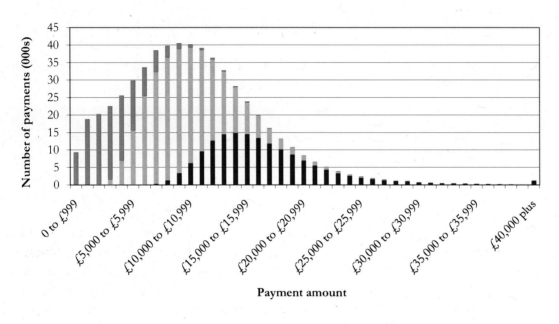

Source: IPSPC analysis of scheme returns data.

Changing landscape of state and private sector pension provision

1.32 There have been fundamental reforms during the last decade both to state pensions and to private sector pensions, in response to challenges such as increasing longevity. The process of change is not yet complete.

State pensions

1.33 The State Pension is traditionally seen as the foundation of pension provision. In response to increased longevity, the State Pension Age is planned to increase over the next four decades. Until April 2010, the State Pension Age was 65 for men and 60 for women. These ages are to be equalised at 65 by 2020 and increased to 66 by 2026, 67 by 2036 and 68 by 2046. At Budget 2010, the Government announced a review of the timetable for increasing the State Pension Age to 66, to take account of increases in longevity and to ensure that the State Pension remains sustainable.

1.34 The basic State Pension and State Second Pension were reformed by the previous Government to increase the numbers eligible. The State Second Pension is set to become a flat-rate top-up to the basic State Pension by around 2030. These changes will significantly increase the numbers of people who receive state pensions and the amounts paid to lower earners.

1.35 The uprating of state pensions to take account of inflation was changed at Budget 2010 in June. In future, the basic State Pension is to be uprated every April by whichever is the highest of: the growth rate of average earnings; the annual increase in the Consumer Price Index (CPI); or 2.5 per cent. As an interim measure, the uprating in April 2011 is to be at least the equivalent of the annual change in the Retail Price Index (RPI). However, the State Second Pension will in future be uprated by CPI, not RPI.[14]

Pensions outside the public sector

1.36 Currently there are about 29 million people working in the UK, with 25 million in employment and the remaining 4 million in self-employed jobs.[15] Of the 19 million private sector employees, about 2.6 million were active members of non-public service DB schemes in 2009. A further million were active members of occupational Defined Contribution (DC) schemes,[16] with another 3 million covered by employer-sponsored group personal pensions or stakeholder pensions, known as 'contract-based' DC schemes.[17] This implies a large gap in coverage, which has increased over time – Chart 1.F shows that close to two thirds of private sector employees lack current employer-sponsored pension provision.

---

14 Current legislation requires public service pensions to be uprated at the same annual rate as the State Second Pension.
15 Labour Market Statistics, ONS, September 2010.
16 Occupational Pension Scheme Survey 2008, Table 2.6.
17 HMRC, Personal and Stakeholder Pensions 2008-09, Tables 7.4 and 7.5.

Chart 1.F: Employer-sponsored pension provision among UK employees

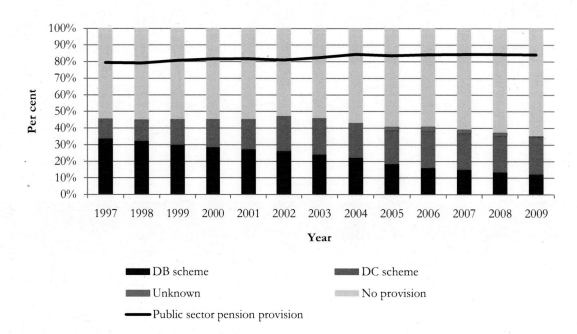

Source: Annual Survey of Hours and Earnings, 2009

Note: There was a methodological change between 2005 and 2006, which has a marginal impact on results. The 'Unknown' category was introduced in 2005.

Private sector landscape

1.37 During much of the 20th century there was substantial convergence in pensions provision between the private and public sectors. This was particularly evident in the first half of the century among employers with large skilled or semi-skilled workforces. By the middle of the century the prevailing consensus was to satisfy demand for skilled labour by offering a steady job with good prospects featuring recruitment at an early age, training and career progression over a 40 to 50 year working life to be rewarded in substantial part by a retirement package offering a pension equivalent to about two thirds of final salary.

1.38 As a result, there are many non-public service DB schemes in the UK. The high point of private sector DB pensions was in the late 1960s, but there was an extended plateau of active DB membership that lasted into the 1990s (Chart 1.G). In 2008, non-public service DB schemes had about 13.1 million members, of whom about 4.9 million were pensioners.[18] But, as described above, only about 2.6 million people are active members of these schemes, with the remainder having a preserved pension entitlement.

---

18 Occupational Pension Scheme Survey 2008, Table 2.3.

Chart 1.G: Non-public service active DB membership

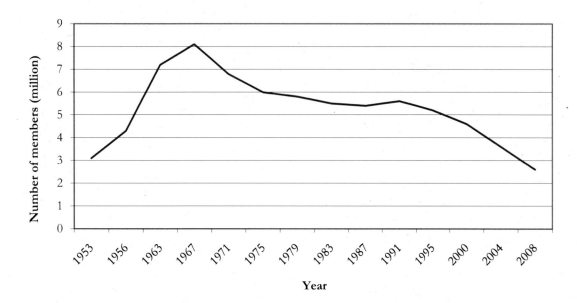

Source: Occupational Pension Scheme Survey, Office for National Statistics.

1.39 The decline in active membership is not because private sector workforces have shrunk overall. It is the coverage of their DB schemes that has shrunk, as private sector employers have shifted to new pension models and remuneration strategies, while the public services have not fundamentally changed their pension provision.

1.40 Many of the remaining DB schemes are now closed to new members. Of the 2.6 million active members of non public service DB schemes in 2008, only 1.1 million were in schemes still open to new members.[19] The other schemes are closed to new entrants and an increasing number of schemes are also closing to new accrual for existing members (see Table 1.D).

Table 1.D: Distribution of members in private sector DB schemes

% of members	2006	2007	2008	2009
Open to new members	64	56	46	38
Closed to new members	34	41	49	57
Closed to all future accruals	2	3	4	5
Winding up	0	0	0	0

Source: The Purple Book, Pensions Regulator, Table 3.4, 2009.

---

19 Occupational Pension Scheme Survey 2008, Table 2.6.

1.41 The contrast between private and public sectors is even more marked than Table 1.D suggests. The figures for non-public service DB schemes include schemes in the wider public sector, such as those for the BBC, Bank of England, Royal Mail and London Underground. Also, the truly private sector DB schemes include schemes carried over when bodies were privatised and new DB schemes provided to workforces transferred to the private sector as a condition of the transfer. Finally, there are some private sector schemes that operate in environments indistinguishable in many ways from the public services and subject to similar influences, such as the Universities Superannuation Scheme.

1.42 Private sector DC arrangements have developed differently, growing steadily as a proportion of total provision. But DC schemes in the public sector are rare, apart from some voluntary pension top up arrangements and the 'Partnership' scheme offered since 2002 to new or re-employed civil servants.

The move to DC schemes in the private sector

1.43 There are several reasons for the migration of many private sector pension schemes from DB to DC. They vary in importance between companies and over time, but two different broad risk categories have been central in many cases.

Investment risks

1.44 In DC systems, the employee carries the investment risk. If investments do not perform well, the member will receive a lower pension. In funded DB schemes the sponsoring employer might be required to make extra contributions to compensate for unexpectedly low investment returns. The corollary of course is that the employer can also benefit from unanticipated funding surpluses in DB schemes, for instance by taking contribution holidays. But many companies, especially smaller ones, have felt unable to bear the level of risk involved.

1.45 The impact of investment risks has been magnified by the move to FRS17 and IAS19 accounting standards over the last decade. The requirement to value pension scheme assets and liabilities at market prices, combined with market volatility, means that the balance sheets of companies with DB pension schemes can vary significantly from year to year, without the position of the company's core business having changed.

Demographic risks

1.46 In DC schemes, the costs of rising longevity are born by employees when they come to buy their annuities; if longevity increases, annuities will become more expensive. In DB schemes, this risk ultimately lies with employers. Past underestimates of longevity have tended to increase employers' costs of providing DB pensions beyond anticipated levels, just as public service pension costs have increased for similar reasons (see Chapter 4).

Future prospects

1.47 There has been a substantial migration away from DB schemes and in particular final salary schemes, in the private sector in the last two decades. But this should not be seen as the last word. Private sector pensions, like those in the public services, are still evolving. It is likely that most schemes will be DC based, with little or no risk sharing. But several large companies are committed to keeping their DB schemes open, often on a career-average basis. Others offer elements of risk sharing for employees through other mechanisms, such as cash balance schemes.

Automatic enrolment

1.48 As shown in Chart 1.F, almost two thirds of private sector employees lack employer-sponsored pension provision. Concerns about the level of saving for retirement led the previous Government to establish a Pensions Commission chaired by Lord Turner. Its reports were published in October 2004 and November 2005.

1.49 In response to these reports, the Government published a White Paper in 2006, which proposed that employees should be automatically enrolled into pension schemes with minimum levels of employer and employee contributions. These new schemes are likely to be almost exclusively DC, with the National Employment Savings Trust (NEST) expected to provide low-cost DC pensions targeted at smaller employers and the low paid. Implementation of automatic enrolment is planned to start from 2012, although the timetable and other details are currently being reviewed.

1.50 The Department for Work and Pensions estimates that between five and nine million employees will begin to participate in employer-sponsored pension schemes as a result of the reforms. Some of the extra enrolment is expected to arise because some people who currently choose not to join an existing pension scheme will opt in. But between 2 and 5 million people are expected to begin to participate due to the provision of new pension opportunities.[20]

---

20 www.dwp.gov.uk/docs/factsheet-impact-reforms-sept09.pdf

2 Recent reforms to public service pensions

Box 2.A: Summary

- The previous Government recognised that public service pensions were in need of reform and began a welcome and necessary modernisation programme when it took office in 1997. In particular, reformed schemes with higher pension ages were introduced for new entrants in most schemes and the introduction of cap and share pension valuations acknowledged that risk needed to be shared more equitably between taxpayers, employers and employees. The present Government has changed future index linking of pensions increases from RPI to CPI.

- However, these reforms have not fully addressed the underlying issues of sustainability and fairness. Although some existing members of some schemes have had increases in their pension ages, to reflect increasing longevity, most have not. Cap and share cannot take account of the increases in cost of pensions over recent decades because people have been living longer. Also, untested, complex cap and share arrangements cannot of themselves, address the underlying issue of structural reforms, nor significantly reduce current costs to taxpayers.

Recent reforms

2.1 The previous Government recognised the need for major reform and began a modernisation programme for public service pensions when it took office in 1997. The first wave of reforms was generally focused on modernising outdated benefit designs. The main changes for the largest seven categories of scheme (NHS, teachers, civil service, local government, armed forces, police and firefighters) are summarised in Table 2.A.

2.2 The uniformed services were among the first to have their pensions reformed. Changes were mainly for new entrants[1] and included a limited increase in pension ages; a reduction in accrual rates; improved management of ill health retirement and the introduction of unmarried partners' pensions. For the police and fire fighters schemes, these changes were implemented together with a reduction in member contributions (for new entrants).

2.3 It has not yet been resolved how to limit employer costs for the uniformed services and several other public service pension schemes by methods such as cap and share (described

---

1 Existing members of the armed forces police and firefighters schemes were given an option to transfer to the new terms and a limited number did. For example, to gain entitlement to unmarried partners pensions.

in Box 2.C), that have been introduced for the biggest schemes. Other schemes, such as the Judicial Pension Scheme, have not been significantly modernised at all.

2.4 The civil service, NHS and teachers schemes across the UK have been modernised to some extent. The Public Services Forum (PSF) Agreement of October 2005 between the previous Government and trades unions allowed existing members to keep a pension age of 60 if they wished, while the pension age for new entrants was set at 65.[2] Other measures included a major transfer of risk from employer to employees through a cap and share mechanism and an increase in employee contribution for the teachers and NHS schemes. For the NHS, tiering of employee contributions by earnings level was introduced.

2.5 The Local Government Pension Schemes were reformed on similar lines, with the addition that pension ages lower than 65 are being phased out by 2020, so compulsory changes to pension ages were not limited to new entrants.[3] The LGPS also introduced tiering of employee contributions by earnings level.

2.6 Many of these reformed schemes changed their accrual rates, in most cases just for new entrants, but all except the civil service are still based on final salary.[4] The civil service scheme instead moved to a career average structure for new entrants. The career average was deemed more appropriate than final salary for an increasingly diverse civil service – one that wished to encourage movement to and from the private sector and to deliver pension outcomes that are more equitable between those individuals whose pay does rise considerably during their civil service careers and those whose pay does not.[5]

2.7 The second wave of reforms including the introduction and implementation of cap and share was in large part aimed at offsetting future cost increases. The most significant reforms in the first and second waves are summarised in Table 2.A.

---

2 Some NHS members will have opted voluntarily to move to the new terms with pension age of 65 as part of the NHS Pensions Choice exercise.

3 This also applied when a higher deferred pension age of 65 was introduced for the armed forces and was applied to existing and new members as part of a package that also increased payments for death in service.

4 The NHS scheme provides final salary pensions for most members but general and dental practitioners have career average arrangements.

5 The accrual rate for the civil service career average arrangements, known as "Nuvos", is 2.3 per cent of annual pensionable pay. This accrual rate compares favourably with many other career average schemes, but the benefit accrued each year before the pension award is now to be uprated by CPI, not RPI or earnings. As Chart 5.G in Chapter 5 indicates, Nuvos is now on average less valuable than the new arrangements for other public service groups.

Table 2.A: Summary of public service pension scheme reforms 2005-08

	NHS[a]	Teachers	Civil service[b]	LGPS (reformed for all members)	Armed forces	Police	Fire
Normal Pension Age (NPA)	60 → 65	60 → 65	60 → 65	Remains 65; Rule of 85 abolished for new service with transitional protection	No change from 55	50 with 25y service (below 50 with 30y); 55 (57 or 60 for higher ranks) → 55	55 (from 50 after 25y service) → 60
NPA for early leavers	Same as NPA	Same as NPA	Same as NPA	Same as NPA	60 → 65 (all members)	60 → 65	60 → 65
Basic design	Remains final salary	Remains final salary	Final salary → Career average	Remains final salary	Remains final salary	Remains final salary	Remains final salary
Accrual rate	80ths → 60ths	80ths → 60ths	60ths → 2.3%	80ths → 60ths	69ths (91ths after 22y[c] → 70ths	60ths (30ths after 20y → 70ths	60ths (30ths after 20y → 70ths
Additional lump sum?	3x pension → commutation	3x pension → commutation	Commutation only	3x pension → commutation	No change from 3x pension	Commutation 4x pension	Commutation only
Late retirement enhancement?	No → Yes	No → Yes	No → Yes	No → Yes	No	No	No
Draw-down option	Yes	Yes (all members)	Yes (all members)	Yes	No	No	No
Rate of employee contributions[d]	6% (5%) → 5-8.5% (for all members)	6% → 6.4% (for all members)	No change from 3.5%	6% (5%) → 5.5%-7.5%	Remains non-contributory	11% → 9.5%	11% → 8.5%
Cost sharing?	Yes	Yes	Yes	Yes	No	No	No
Eligibility for survivor's pension	Now includes non-legal partners and payable for life (but only for new joiners in the police and fire schemes						
Survivor's pension on death in retirement	Remains a 160ths pension	Remains a 160ths pension	160ths → 3/8ths of member's pension	Remains a 160ths pension	50% → 62.5% of member's pension	Remains a 50% member's pension	Remains a 50% member's pension
Ill-health benefit	1-tier → 2-tier	1-tier → 2-tier	Remains 2-tier	1-tier → 3-tier (proposed)	1-tier → 2-tier	1-tier → 2-tier	Remains 2-tier
Timescale	1 Apr 2008	1 Jan 2007	30 Jul 2007	1 April 2008	6 April 2005	6 April 2006	6 April 2006

Source: PPI.

41

Notes for Table 2.A

a The scheme for salaried staff is illustrated. Self-employed members, such as GPs and Dentists, have a career-average scheme that is not shown.

b The Premium section of the civil service scheme is illustrated here, since the Classic section has been closed to new members since 2002.

c For other ranks. Officers have higher accrual rates.

d If a range is shown then employee contributions depend on pay. Figures in brackets denote special provisions for certain categories of workers.

Further notes:

Normal pension age in the first row is NPA for active members.

The LGPS employee rates shown are for E & W and Northern Ireland; rates in Scotland are different.

AFPS early pensions or their equivalent are still available from around age 40.

The old AFPS scheme uses "representative pay" for those below one star rank – Brigadier or equivalent. That is only roughly equivalent to final salary, as it is based on the average pay for a member of that rank with a particular number of years of service.

Pensions for life regardless of remarriage etc do not apply to dependants' pensions under the civil service "Classic" arrangements or the old armed forces arrangements as well as to the old police and firefighters schemes.

The savings assumed from reforms

2.8 The overall cost savings from these reforms, compared with the costs that might otherwise have arisen, vary considerably between schemes. Over the next 30 years, expected savings under the reforms of the uniformed service schemes range from under a tenth of overall cost for the armed forces to about a fifth for police and a third for firefighters.[6] However, the savings will build up gradually, in line with the gradual increase in the proportion of members accruing benefits under the new pension terms. Consequently, because of protections for existing members' past and future service, overall costs for these schemes are predicted to remain at over a third of pensionable pay for much of the next decade.[7]

2.9 Across the four largest categories of scheme (local government, civil service, NHS and teachers) cost savings from the reforms, compared with what costs might have been, may be equivalent to five per cent or more of overall scheme cost by the 2040s.[8] This estimate excludes any allowance for the possible effects at future pension scheme valuations of new arrangements for risk transfer (cap and share).

2.10 However, as with the uniformed services, because of protections given to existing members in respect of future service, it will be some time before the full impact of the reforms

6 About 2 per cent of pay for armed forces, 7 per cent of pay for police and 12 per cent of pay for firefighters, measured in terms of the scheme standard contribution rate, based on IPSPC analysis of information published in answer to PQs etc.
7 Based on PPI and IPSPC analysis of GAD valuation reports.
8 Based on estimates provided for schemes by GAD, and measured in terms of the standard scheme contribution rate giving 1.2 per cent of pay for civil service and NHS and 1.3 per cent of pay for teachers and LGPS. The savings are based on comparisons with what the employer contribution costs might have been if the reforms had not been implemented, not allowing for cap and share.

appears in employer contribution rates. Also, some of those savings may be offset by future increases in employer costs rather than being reductions from the current levels of cost.[9]

2.11 The 2009 Pre-Budget Report (PBR) and the long-term public finance report (LTPFR) included an allowance for further savings to those discussed above, if further longevity pressures were as then anticipated and if the 'second wave' cap and share reforms were rigorously implemented. It was assumed that two-thirds of the savings through cap and share would be met by benefit reductions, with the other third leading to contribution increases. The PBR assumed a saving of about £1billion a year on account of increases in employee contributions resulting from cap and share from April 2012. The 2009 LTPFR indicated possible savings through reductions in benefits of £2 billion or more a year in the very long-term across the NHS, teachers and civil service pension schemes in a 'central scenario'.[10]

CPI indexation

2.12 The cost savings figures discussed above do not allow for the change to indexation by movements in the CPI rather than the RPI, for upratings from April 2011, that was announced at the Budget 2010 in June. That change is expected to produce upratings that may be on average about three-quarters of a percentage point lower than the equivalent RPI figure for that year.[11]

> **Box 2.B: Indexation**
>
> - The uprating of public service pensions is linked by an Act of Parliament to the uprating of the State Second Pension. Since 1988, the State Second Pension has been increased by the annual movement in the September RPI.[a] At Budget 2010 in June the Government said that the CPI represented a better measure of inflation for most pensions and benefits, including State Second Pension and public service pensions; and would be used in future.
>
> a The September RPI was also used for the 1987 uprating but that was not based on the movement in a full year. Between 1979 and 1987 the arrangements for uprating State Second Pensions were based on movements in the actual or forecast RPI for months other than September. Before the introduction of the State Earnings-Related Pension Scheme in 1979 public service pension upratings were separately linked to movements in the RPI.

2.13 The Budget 2010 projected that the change to CPI uprating would save £1.8 billion a year across the unfunded schemes by 2015-16, continuing to rise for many decades.

---

9 For example, in the NHS, where it was expected that employer contribution rates would otherwise increase by about 2 per cent of pay over the next 15-20 years on account of better careers and pay progression.

10 The outcomes were highly dependent on the longevity assumptions used in the different scenarios.

11 The difference in the underlying methodology for compiling the CPI, which allows for substitution of goods and services by others of a comparable type as they become relatively more expensive, would produce a difference of about half a percentage point a year. The current exclusion of most housing costs from the CPI would account for the other quarter of a percentage point a year. The difference between CPI and RPI because of the exclusion of housing costs is however forecast at present to be greater than a quarter of a percentage point for some of the next few years, so the overall effect across those years exceeds three-quarters of a percentage point a year.

2.14 If CPI uprating were to be continued through the 21st century, with an average differential from RPI of 0.75 percentage points as forecast, then subject to how cap and share is operated, this change could reduce public service pension expenditure by over 10 per cent by 2030 (£5 billion in 2008-09 prices) and by 20 per cent by 2060 (£20 billion in 2008-09 prices). There is further analysis of the possible long-term effects in Chapter 4, for example in paragraphs 4.31 to 4.34, Table 4.C and Chart 4.A.

Overall impact

2.15 Separate analysis from the Pensions Policy Institute (PPI), explored more fully in Chapter 5, has considered the value of the pre and post reform schemes to members after allowing for the CPI change.[12] This analysis, summarised in Table 2.B, suggests that the change in indexation measure may have reduced the value to scheme members by around 15 per cent on average. When this change is combined with other reforms to date across the major schemes the value to current members of reformed schemes with CPI indexation is on average 25 per cent less than the pre-reform schemes with RPI indexation. However, these measures will take many decades to fully affect the costs of pensions in payment, which are heavily influenced by existing pensioners, the vast majority of whom are still on pre-reform benefit structures schemes.

Table 2.B: Recent evolution of average effective employee benefit rates for the main schemes

Average employee benefit rates	Members of old schemes – % of pay	Members of new schemes – % of pay
with RPI indexation		
NHS, teachers, LGPS, civil service	23	20
All 7 main public service pension schemes	24	21
(NHS, teachers, LGPS, civil service, police, fire and armed forces)		
with CPI indexation (from April 2011)		
NHS, teachers, LGPS, civil service	19	17
All 7 main public service pension schemes	20	18
(NHS, teachers, LGPS, civil service, police, fire and armed forces)		

Source: PPI.

2.16 The scale of the change in value varies considerably between schemes, with the largest difference in cost between old and new schemes applying to the schemes for the civil service

---

12 PPI measure this in terms of 'effective employee benefit rates', using a corporate bond discount rate (see Chapters 4 and 5) and allowing for the reforms implemented up to 2008 and the change to CPI indexation, but not possible future effects of cap and share.

and the uniformed services and the smallest to the LGPS (in part because the LGPS applied changes in pension ages to many existing members). The differences between schemes are considered further in Chapter 5, for example in Chart 5.G.

Building on cap and share

2.17 At present cap and share applies to the 'big four' categories of scheme – NHS, teachers, civil service and local government.[13] It seems that an underlying policy intention was to keep the levels of employer cost no higher than those reached around 2004 and 2005. The caps for teachers, NHS and civil service employer contributions appear to have been set with that in mind.

Box 2.C: Cap and share

Cap and share are arrangements for sharing and limiting costs introduced following the Public Services Forum Agreement of October 2005. Under cap and share, increases or reductions in cost pressures identified at a pension scheme actuarial valuation are shared between employees and employers, up to the value of a cap. Above that cap the increases or reductions are borne by employees, either by changing employee contributions or the cost of employee benefits (by measures such as changing pension ages), or by doing both. Below that cap, increases or reductions are shared between employers and employees.

2.18 The caps were to be taken into account in the next round of scheme actuarial valuations. Every three or four years such valuations will assess the current financial position of each scheme and highlight any cost pressures to be met by extra employer and employee contributions or reductions in benefits. The current cost caps and employer contribution rates are shown in Table 2.C.

---

13 It also applies to the Parliamentary Pension Scheme, which has undertaken a cap and share valuation.

Table 2.C: Current cost caps and employer contribution rates in the four biggest schemes

Scheme	Valuation date (as at)	Cost cap as % of pensionable pay	Current employer contribution rate
Teachers E & W	March 2008	14	14.1
NHS E & W	March 2008	14.2 (and 14)[a]	14
PCSPS	March 2010	20[b]	18.9[c]
LGPS E & W	March 2010	Not yet fixed[d]	c13.2[e]

Source: Pension schemes.

a The NHSPS England and Wales has an interim cost cap of 14.2 per cent for the current valuation, as at March 2008, but moves to 14 per cent for the next valuation, as at March 2012.

b The PCSPS rate of 20 per cent was set taking account of the different level of employer and employee contributions and at a time when the average PCSPS employer rate was 19.5 per cent, before the reduction to 18.9 per cent following the 2007 valuation.

c This is a weighted average of the actual employer rates that vary, by pay band, from 16.7 per cent to 24.3 per cent.

d The LGPS has used an indicative rate of 13.2 per cent for certain purposes, but that pre-dated more recent information about the 2007 LGPS England and Wales valuation results.

e The 13.2 per cent figure was based on a notional national model fund valuation using 2007 data and excludes the investment surpluses and deficits on individual local authority pension funds. The need to look across 89 separate fund valuations in England and Wales and exclude investment surpluses and deficits makes it difficult to derive an overall England and Wales scheme cost and employer rate equivalent to that for the unfunded schemes.

2.19 Cost sharing provisions are also in place for the Northern Ireland Civil Service Scheme, and the teachers and NHS schemes in both Scotland and Northern Ireland but they have 'capping by proxy'. This means there is no specific employer contribution rate cap for these devolved administration schemes. Their employer rate would be determined by taking the overall cost determined at their scheme valuation and deducting the employee rate as determined under the cap and share rules for the PCSPS UK, teachers England and Wales or NHS England and Wales. The intention is to maintain commonality of pension provision and mobility across all these occupational groups.[14]

2.20 There are, however, some cost reductions or pressures that are not necessarily shared under the cap and share provisions. For example, the effects of changes in financial assumptions such as prices and discount rates might not be shared with employees under cap and share provisions. The cost sharing terms also vary from scheme to scheme, so for example savings from pension age of 65 for new entrants fall only to employers in the teachers and civil service schemes, but are shared in the NHS scheme.

---

14 The rules for the NHS and teachers schemes in Scotland and Northern Ireland provide that if this results in much higher employer rates than the equivalent schemes in England and Wales, it is possible to review how the contribution rates are set. But it would then be necessary to bear in mind the potential major implications for staff mobility, careers and ability to fill key posts in those occupational groups if employee contribution rates and pension benefits diverged significantly.

2.21 As Table 2.C shows, at the moment the employer contribution rate for the teachers England and Wales scheme is above its cap, for the NHS England and Wales scheme it is just below and the civil service is approaching its cap.

2.22 At present the LGPS does not yet have a cap in England and Wales or specific provisions for capping in Scotland or Northern Ireland.[15] It is uncertain whether the employer rates resulting from LGPS cap and share valuations would be above or below the sort of cap that might be set.

2.23 The cap and share provisions for the LGPS will be particularly complicated because of the devolved structure of the scheme, with 89 separate funds in England and Wales; and because the effects of funding are to be excluded from the sharing arrangements. The LGPS cap would be based on a notional (model) fund valuation that excluded investment surpluses and deficits and the cap and share valuation used to determine employee contribution rates across the scheme would also be a notional fund valuation.

The limitations of cap and share

2.24 Many schemes are not yet covered by cap and share arrangements and even where they are, cap and share is an untried system. Some basic principles have been agreed, but the arrangements are still in the developmental stage. Processes are still being worked out even where provision for cap and share has been made in scheme rules.

2.25 Cap and share has other limitations:

- cap and share reduces scheme costs only if scheme valuations reveal future additional cost pressures compared with a recent baseline (which is usually the preceding valuation). Therefore, although cap and share can reduce scheme costs below what they might have been, it would not at present deal with the very considerable increases in the costs of providing pensions, worth several percent of pay a year, that have resulted from increases in longevity in recent decades;

- in order to pick up past increases in longevity within cap and share it would be necessary either to set a baseline reflecting costs three or four decades ago, when longevity began to rise much more markedly, or to reduce the employer contribution rate caps to levels well below the employer rates that have been paid in recent years;

- operating cap and share on a scheme-by-scheme basis seems unlikely to produce coherent outcomes across government. Those outcomes would include what members of different schemes pay for a comparable benefit, what benefit designs are offered and how risk to taxpayers, employers and members is managed; and

---

15 LGPS Scotland has been undertaking discussions but provisions have not been finalised for their fund valuations in 2011. The LGPS in Northern Ireland is awaiting developments in England and Wales; and Scotland.

- under current cap and share valuation processes, changes in costs[16] are attributed to members and employers, including those in the private sector. Under the current methodology for calculating scheme costs at cap and share valuations, overall costs to be shared at the next valuations may be much lower than previously expected. Cap and share may therefore not of itself produce the anticipated results, including the reductions in overall pressures on public spending and finance that are summarised in paragraph 2.12.

2.26 All this means that cap and share on its own will not deliver the type of wide-ranging structural reforms that are needed or significant reductions in current costs for taxpayers. It would instead be necessary to apply a more coherent overall policy framework when determining future pension provision and how levels of employer cost and risk are assessed, managed and taken into account in overall remuneration.

16 This would include where costs and savings had arisen from changes in the costs of paying existing pensioners.

The Principles

Independent
Public Service
Pensions Commission

3 The framework of principles

> **Box 3.A: Summary**
>
> This section of the report is structured around the framework of principles that the Commission has developed. Public service pensions should be:
>
> - affordable and sustainable;
>
> - adequate and fair;
>
> - support productivity; and
>
> - transparent and simple.
>
> The principles have been chosen to provide a balanced and comprehensive framework with which to consider the case for reform and against which to assess the options for long-term structural change.
>
> The principles will tend to pull in different directions. This will help make the trade-offs clear so that a sensible overall judgement can be reached.

3.1 This section of the report is structured around the Commission's four main principles for public service pensions. The principles have been chosen to provide a balanced and comprehensive framework with which to consider the case for reform, as we do in this interim report and against which to assess the options for long-term structural reform, which the Commission will do in the final report. This set of principles echo a number of the areas for consideration that were identified in our terms of reference and also reflect the full range of issues covered in the evidence the Commission received. They have been chosen because the Commission considers them to be the most important factors that should govern the overall design of public service pensions: affordable and sustainable; adequate and fair; support productivity; and transparent and simple.

Affordable and sustainable

3.2 Spending on public service pensions must be affordable and must remain affordable over time to be sustainable. What level of pension cost is affordable is a political decision for the Government within the context of a range of priorities. But it is not an issue that can just be looked at in the short-term as the effects of decisions taken on pensions tend to build up and then persist over a long period. In assessing affordability and sustainability the Commission has identified a range of relevant cost measures to consider and the need for an agreed discount rate. Part of any assessment of cost must include the consequences of any reform on increased take-up of benefits such as pension credit. Critical to sustainability is the sensitivity of future costs to risks, such as changes to longevity and how these risks are managed and shared. Options for change must deliver an affordable and sustainable system with the robustness and flexibility to withstand the uncertainties of the future.

Adequate and fair

3.3 Public service pensions should provide an adequate level of retirement income for public service workers with a reasonable degree of certainty. To assess reforms against this principle the Commission needs an agreed measure of what is adequate and what should be measured against the benchmark. The Commission provides some ideas in this interim report. Adequacy is a measure of fairness, but the Commission is also looking at fairness in the distribution of contributions and benefits between members of the same pension scheme – by income, by career path, by time of entry; fairness between different schemes; fairness between generations of taxpayers; and fairness between the taxpayer and the public service employee.

Support productivity

3.4 To support productivity, public service pension scheme design should be consistent with an efficient labour market for employees so that the taxpayer can be confident that public services are being delivered on a value for money basis. In general, scheme design should avoid barriers to the movement of employees between sectors. This needs to be viewed in the context of the whole remuneration package and whether the schemes support the recruitment and retention of the right people in the right jobs in a cost-effective way and be able to deal flexibly with specific job issues. In particular, they should not be an unintended barrier to the outsourcing and mutualisation of public services that could drive greater productivity and efficiency in public services.

Transparent and simple

3.5 Public service pensions should be widely understood, both by the scheme members with regard to their own specific entitlements and possible future benefits and by taxpayers who have a role in funding the schemes. The key design features and the costs to employers and employees need to be set out clearly and transparently. It follows that public service pension design should be relatively easy to understand and proposals set out with the aim of obtaining wide agreement. Assessment of reform needs to consider potential trade-offs together with implementation and transitional issues including the means for protecting accrued rights and possibilities for more cost-effective administration. It is also important that public service pension schemes, like schemes in the private sector, have a clear legal framework and a governance structure that provides clarity on the roles of the interested parties.

53

How the principles will be used

3.6 These principles will form the basis for assessing the long-term options for reform. The evidence in this interim report has been framed around the principles and reference has been made to their relevance to the Commission's final report.

3.7 It is not intended to weight the principles, or the evidence associated with them and consequently the Commission's final report will necessarily be subjective. It is highly likely that some of the principles will be in conflict as varying options for reform are examined more closely. For example a scheme that delivers an adequate level of retirement income and is calibrated to meet objectives on fairness may as a result be difficult to understand, contrary to the principle of transparency and simplicity. Therefore, all options for change will have to be assessed against each of the principles and a balance struck. The intention is for the trade-offs to be clear so that a sensible judgement can be reached.

Affordable and sustainable

Box 4.A: Summary

- The long-term and uncertain nature of public service pensions makes assessing 'cost' very difficult, whether this involves deciding what measure to use or how that should be calculated. Government, employers and commentators use many different measures.

- Considering the projected future benefit expenditure as a percentage of GDP can be a useful tool in assessing affordability over the longer-term. Based on the latest figures produced by the Government Actuary's Department, which take account of latest developments including the move to CPI indexation, public service pension benefit expenditure from unfunded schemes is expected to reach 1.9 per cent of GDP in 2010-11 and remain close to this level for the next decade before decreasing to 1.4 per cent of GDP by 2060. These projections are dependent on the assumptions made, especially in the longer-term.

- Improvements in longevity mean that pensioners are in receipt of pension payments for longer making these schemes significantly more costly than was expected when they were set up. Further improvements in longevity are expected but the rate of improvement is uncertain – in the past improvements have been consistently underestimated. Sustainable pension schemes in the public sector need to have mechanisms to manage such uncertainties in future costs.

- The discount rate used to set employer and employee contributions is critical in order to ensure that the costs of the future pension promises are being adequately allowed for in workforce planning and budgeting and that contributions required can be appropriately divided between the employer and the employee. The Commission believes there is a case for reviewing the current discount rate of RPI plus 3.5 per cent, which is clearly at the high end of the spectrum and recommends that the Government undertakes a review to establish the appropriate rate, preferably in time to inform the Commission's final report.

- Most public service pension schemes are unfunded. The Commission's view is that, given the risks, the lack of obvious economic benefit and the large transition costs of moving to a funded basis, this remains appropriate as the basic financing model.

Box 4.A (continued): Summary

- The Local Government Pension Scheme (LGPS) is in a different position as it is funded. Its costs are in addition to those expressed above as a percentage of GDP. However, the funds are not operated on the basis of trust law or subject to the same funding and regulatory requirements that apply to the generality of funded schemes. The LGPS is unlikely to be fully funded for the foreseeable future, although switching to CPI indexation will improve its funding levels. The Commission has concluded that the current LGPS should continue on a funded basis. In any event, holding investment funds does not remove the need to consider structural reforms to deal with issues around the sustainability and fairness of benefits – issues common to all public service pension schemes.

- In considering reform, the Commission seeks to avoid changes that would make recipients significantly more reliant on state help.

4.1 Ensuring that public service pensions are affordable and sustainable is crucial but ultimately, the level of spending on public service pensions is a decision for Government. Sustainability relates to how pension payments are expected to change and whether costs are manageable in the long-term, as well as considering the impact of different risks in the system on the variability of future costs and who faces these risks.

Present and future cost

Methods for measuring the cost of unfunded public service pensions

4.2 Pensions are complex and uncertain in nature. The 'cost' of pension schemes is a difficult concept to define and measure, especially where the schemes are unfunded. Here the Commission considers some of the measures that can be used when considering the cost of public service pension schemes.

Box 4.B: Terms used in discussing the cost of unfunded public service pension schemes

Net cash expenditure	Benefits paid to recipients less contributions received by central government from employees and employers in any one year.

Figures published in Resource Accounts/local authority accounts:
Calculated on assumptions broadly comparable with private sector accounting practice.

• **Accrued liabilities**	A measure of the value, in today's money, of all pension entitlements to be paid in the future that have been earned to date.
• **Current service cost**	A measure of the value of the new pension promises built up over a year.
• **Interest cost**	A measure of the amount by which the value of accrued liabilities increases over a year as a result of the "unwinding" of the discount rate, reflecting the fact that pension payments are closer to being paid.

Standard/current contribution rates published in actuarial valuations:
Typically assessed every 3 or 4 years as part of the SCAPE[a] valuation process using a discount rate of 3.5 per cent above RPI inflation.

• **Standard contribution rate**	The total rate of contributions (employer plus employee) which would need to be paid in order to meet the cost of pension benefits accruing over a defined period, expressed as a percentage of payroll.
• **Current contribution rate**	The standard contribution rate as adjusted for past surpluses and deficits and payable by employers and employees.
Future benefit payments as a percentage of GDP	Projected future cash benefit outgo expressed as a percentage of projected future GDP. This can be expressed gross or net of member contributions.

a SCAPE (Superannuation Contributions adjusted for Past Experience) is a methodology used to set employer contribution rates across public service. It is intended to mirror the operation of a funded scheme by keeping track of a notional 'Pension Account'. Under the SCAPE approach, employer contribution rates are set as: The standard contribution rate, less the employee contribution rate adjusted to reflect any surplus/deficit in the Pension Account at the review date.

4.3 All of the measures listed in Box 4.B can tell us something about the cost of pensions but each must be taken in context and interpreted with care. In particular, they are each appropriate for a particular purpose and may not be the most relevant for the consideration of the affordability and sustainability of public service pension schemes.

4.4 A number of the measures discussed require a discount rate[1] in order to express future expenditure in today's money. The appropriate discount rate to use for each purpose has been the subject of much debate and this is discussed in detail later in this chapter.

Net cash expenditure

4.5 Net cash expenditure reports how much the Government pays out in benefit payments each year over and above the level of contributions coming in. In June 2010 the Office for Budget Responsibility (OBR) reported that net expenditure on public service pensions payments (excluding the local government, police and firefighters pension schemes) was set to grow as shown in Table 4.A below.[2] The OBR explained that expenditure under this measure is expected to increase over this period primarily because of a larger number of pensioners, an increase in how long people are living and past real terms increases in earnings. The Government's pay restraint policy is also expected to have an impact, since in the short-term it reduces contributions but has little effect on total pension payments.

Table 4.A: OBR Budget 2010 forecast: net cash expenditure

Year	Net cash expenditure (£bn)	Benefit payments (£bn)	Contributions received (£bn)
2008-09	3.1	22.5	19.4
2009-10 (estimate)	3.1	24.3	21.2
2010-11 (forecast)	4.0	25.4	21.3
2011-12 (forecast)	5.1	26.8	21.6
2012-13 (forecast)	5.8[a]	28.3	21.5
2013-14 (forecast)	7.3[a]	29.9	21.5
2014-15 (forecast)	8.9[a]	31.3	21.4
2015-16 (forecast)	10.3[a]	32.9	21.6

Source. OBR

a Forecasts from 2012-13 onwards include a £1 billion saving from cap and share.

4.6 The growing gap between contributions in and payments out in the coming years has been the subject of much discussion. The increase in net expenditure in Table 4.A may seem

---

1 Box 4.D explains briefly how discount rates are used.

2 Budget 2010: The economy & public finances, supplementary material Table 2.3, June 2010, Office for Budget Responsibility, www.budgetresponsibility.independent.gov.uk/d/junebudget_supplementary_material.pdf. Forecast expenditure in 2010-11 reflects actuarial advice on the rate and level at which benefits are expected to come into payment, the rate of future employer and employee contributions and the latest information relating to scheme demographics.

steep but this is the difference in two much larger numbers and as such is inherently volatile – the increase in benefit payments does not see such a steep increase. The growing gap is a consequence of an unfunded system where the balance between active members, who generally contribute to schemes and pensioner members, who receive benefits, is changing over time as explained in more detail in Box 1.B in Chapter 1. In particular, the growing gap reflects the forecast fall in public service workforce numbers, and therefore active members of public service pension schemes paying contributions over the next few years. Active member contributions are based on the future benefits they themselves are expected to receive rather than on current pensioner benefit levels.

4.7 This measure can in a limited way highlight cash flow issues for government that could affect other expenditure in the short-term however it does not provide a complete picture of long-term affordability.

Accrued liabilities

4.8 The Government Actuary's Department (GAD) has estimated the accrued liability for all unfunded public service pension schemes at £770 billion, at 31 March 2008. This figure represents all pension entitlements that have accrued[3] at the date of calculation and which will fall due for payment over the next seven to eight decades in a single measure. It is not a sum of money that will ever be needed at one time.

4.9 Using liability values can increase transparency and aid comparability. Valuations of liabilities for public service pensions are useful for making comparisons with private sector schemes. However, the inherently large public service numbers must be taken in context, as one of many long-term Government commitments, alongside future health and education costs and the basic State Pension; and one that will be paid over a period of 70 years or more. Also, as it is based on benefits earned to date, largely already fixed, liability values cannot provide information on the affordability of pension benefits to be earned in the future over which the Government has control.

4.10 Liability values are sensitive to the assumptions used and in particular to the discount rate. The discount rate used for Resource Accounts is based on AA corporate bond yields, broadly in line with the private sector accounting practices. This yield is volatile, fluctuating with movements in the market, making the liability values also very volatile. Calculations by Towers Watson have estimated more recent total accrued liability figures for all unfunded schemes and public service pension schemes (on methodology consistent with the 31 March 2008 figure) as follows:

---

3 As this treats the scheme as an ongoing entity, it allows for future growth in pensionable earnings for those members who are currently contributing – the 'active' members.

Table 4.B: Accrued liability estimates[a]

Source	Discount rate (above RPI inflation)	31 March 2008 (£bn)	31 March 2009 (£bn)	31 March 2010 (£bn)
HMT	AA corporate bond yields (2.5% in 2008)	770		
Towers Watson	AA corporate bond yields (3.2% in 2009, 1.8% in 2010)		728	993

Source: LTPFR, November 2009 and Towers Watson press release 22 March 2010.

a Note these figures do not take into account the recently announced change in indexation method.

4.11 The accrued liability figure as at 31 March 2009 was lower than the 31 March 2008 figure primarily because a higher discount rate was used (which reduces accrued liabilities as it places a lower value on pension payments in the future). The following year the reverse was true.

4.12 The changes in the discount rate assumptions over this period did not result from adjustments to the assumed security or generosity of public service pensions. Instead, as they were linked to AA corporate bond yields they reflected the change in assumed risk of corporate defaults during and after the credit crunch. A change of this kind in bond yields has no implications for the actual cost of providing public service pensions, so such estimates of accrued liabilities need to be used with caution.

Current service cost and interest cost

4.13 The cost of pensions reported in annual accounts consists mainly of the current service cost and the interest cost.[4] Current service costs represent the 'new' pension entitlements earned over any one year. The Office for Budget Responsibility estimated the current service cost for all unfunded public service pension schemes at around £26 billion for the year ending 31 March 2008.[5] As with the value of accrued liabilities, this is a single figure representation of pension payments that will be paid 70 years or more into the future.

4.14 Interest cost can be thought of as the increase in the value of liabilities as a result of the benefits being one year closer to being paid (they are discounted for one year less which increases the present cost). Current service costs and interest costs are calculated on an AA corporate bond yield discount rate and so subject to the same market volatility as accrued liabilities.

4.15 This volatility is illustrated in published figures for the current service cost and interest cost for all unfunded schemes (excluding the police and firefighters schemes) as follows:

---

4 Current service cost is charged to operating profit, interest cost to other financing income.
5 Office for Budget Responsibility, Pre-Budget forecast, paragraph 5.41, June 2010.

Table 4.C: Current service cost and interest cost

Year	Current service cost (£bn)	Interest cost (£bn)
2004-05	15.3	24.1
2005-06	20.9	27.4
2006-07	21.1	29.5
2007-08	24.5	32.8
2008-09	24.8[a]	36.5
2009-10 (expected)	23.9	37.8
2010-11 (forecast)	32.8	41.1

Source: Public Expenditure Statistical Analyses, Annex D, Table D1, HM Treasury, 2010.

a This is slightly different from the £26bn figure quoted in Paragraph 4.14 as it does not include the police or firefighters pension schemes.

Standard contribution rates

4.16 Standard contribution rates[6] calculated through scheme valuations are used to set current contribution rates and therefore what employers actually pay each year once employee contributions are taken into account. When applied to the pensionable payroll, standard contribution rates can measure the additional pension entitlements earned in each year.

4.17 The fact that the amount actually paid by employers and employees often differs from the current service cost discussed above can cause confusion as both are designed to represent the cost of benefits accruing over a certain period. For example, Table 4.D compares the amounts paid by employees and employers and the current service cost for the Teachers' Pension Scheme over recent years. Similar results can be shown for other schemes.

---

6 The current contribution rate actually used is the standard contribution rate adjusted for (notional) surpluses and deficits

Table 4.D: Comparison of contributions paid and current service costs in Teachers' Pension Scheme

Year	2006-07	2007-08	2008-09	2009-10
Employee contributions paid (£bn)[a]	1.3	1.4	1.5	1.5
Employer contributions paid (£bn)[a]	2.8	3.0	3.1	3.2
Total contributions paid (£bn) [a]	4.1	4.4	4.6	4.7
Current service cost (£bn)[b]	5.0	6.7	5.8	5.0
Current service cost less total contributions paid (£bn)	0.9	2.3	1.2	0.3
Discount rate used to calculate current service cost, above RPI inflation (%)[b]	2.8	1.8	2.5	3.2

Source: IPSPC analysis of Resource Accounts.

a Discount rate used to calculate contributions is 3.5% above RPI inflation (SCAPE).

b Service costs calculated on discount rates at year start.

4.18 Over this period the current service cost of pensions accrued in each year has been higher than the contributions paid. The difference between the figures in each year arises mainly because the discount rate used to calculate the current service cost has been lower than that used to set contribution rates (currently based on a fixed rate of 3.5 per cent per annum above RPI inflation) and has therefore placed a higher value on pensions which will be paid in the future. The difference is not necessarily a problem. The figures discussed are used for different purposes and as such are calculated on assumptions deemed appropriate to each purpose.

Cost projections

4.19 To assess the sustainability of public service pensions, it is useful to consider projections of benefit payments in the future. The National Audit Office's March 2010 report The Cost of Public Service Pensions considered the public service pension benefit projections set out in HM Treasury's Long-term public finance report in December 2009. These covered all unfunded public service pension schemes and are summarised on various measures in Table 4.E.

Table 4.E: Public service pensions benefit projections

Year	2009-10	2019-20	2029-30	2039-40	2049-50	2059-60
Constant 2008-09 prices (£bn)	25.4	35.1	44.2	53.3	63.4	79.1
Constant 2008-09 earnings (£bn)	24.9	28.2	29.2	28.9	28.2	28.8
% of GDP	1.7	1.9	1.9	1.8	1.7	1.7

Source: NAO and HM Treasury.

4.20 In constant price terms (i.e. allowing for RPI inflation over the period), public service pension benefit payments were projected to rise from £25.4 billion in 2009-10 to £79.1 billion in 2059-60. While this appears a significant increase, it does not take account of the expectation that earning levels across the economy as a whole, including the public service, will increase by more than RPI inflation in the long-term. Adjusting these figures for constant earning levels shows a more gradual increase from £24.9 billion in 2009-10 to £29.2 billion in 2029-30, with payments remaining around that level thereafter.

4.21 The final measure considered was public service pension benefit payments as a percentage of projected GDP. Since benefits are mainly financed ultimately through taxation and tax revenues are closely related to GDP, this is an attractive measure when looking at long-term affordability as it can be regarded as a proxy measure for the country's ability to pay public service pensions in the future.

4.22 On this measure, public service pension benefit payments were forecast by the OBR to rise from 1.7 per cent of GDP in 2009-10 to 1.9 per cent of GDP in 2019-20 and 2029-30, before falling back to 1.7 per cent by 2049-50.

4.23 Projections of public service pension expenditure were compared with projections for other age-related expenditure in the OBR's PBR forecast in June 2010 and have been reproduced in Table 4.F.

Table 4.F: Age-related expenditure as a percentage of GDP

Year	2009-10	2019-20	2029-30	2039-40	2049-50
Public service pensions	1.8	1.9	1.9	1.8	1.7
Health	8.0	8.5	9.3	10.0	10.3
Long-term care	1.2	1.4	1.7	1.9	2.1
State pensions	5.5	5.3	5.9	6.5	6.5
Education	6.0	5.9	6.0	5.8	5.7

Source: Pre-Budget forecast, Office for Budget Responsibility, Table 5.1, June 2010.

4.24 Given the factors discussed above, the Commission's view is that projected public service pension benefit payments as a percentage of estimated GDP is an effective measure of the future cost of public service pensions and the Commission focuses on this measure in the following paragraphs.

Long-term costs

4.25 Building on the figures shown in Table 4.E, the Commission has asked GAD to provide updated projections of future benefit payments from unfunded public service pension schemes in light of developments since these figures were published. There were three key updates allowing for: the change in pensions indexation from RPI to CPI, the short-term pay freeze and public service workforce projections as set out by the OBR in July 2010 and an introduction of a longer term public service workforce growth assumption of

0.25 per cent per annum (compared with 0 per cent assumed in Table 4.E). A summary of this analysis including more detail about the assumptions used can be found in Annex B. In particular, the allowance for switching to CPI indexation uses the most recent OBR forecasts of RPI and CPI up to 2015 and a differential between the two measures of 0.75 per cent per annum thereafter.

4.26 The results of their revised analysis have been incorporated with GDP forecasts consistent with both the GDP projections set out in the OBR's Budget 2010 forecast[7] and the projections of future benefit payments. The results are illustrated in the Chart 4.A, together with outturns since 1999-2000.

Chart 4.A: Projected benefit payments as a percentage of GDP – central projection

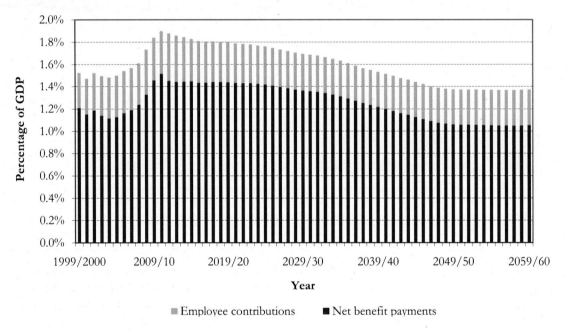

Source: GAD projections for IPSPC and IPSPC analysis.

4.27 The analysis shows that total benefit payments are expected to peak at 1.9 per cent of GDP in 2010-11 and remain at about 1.8 per cent of GDP for the following decade before falling to around 1.4 per cent of GDP by 2059-60. Net of employee contributions, benefit payments peak at about 1.5 per cent of GDP in 2010-11, before falling to below 1.1 per cent by 2059-60.

4.28 There has been a sizeable increase in benefit payments as a percentage of GDP over the last decade. This has been driven mainly by the increase in the number of public service pensioners (both as a result of an increased public service workforce and pensioners living longer), which increased cash payments out and the recent recession, which reduced the size

---

7 Budget forecast, OBR, June 2010.

of GDP. This increasing trend is expected to peak at 2010-11 after which, pension benefits paid are expected to continue to increase (in real terms) but at a slower rate than GDP.

4.29 The projections show differences from the previous figures in Table 4.E published in the December 2009 long-term public finance report (and subsequently analysed by the NAO in their March 2010 report) as a result of the updates made to the assumptions:

- allowing for the change in pensions indexation from RPI to the CPI serves to reduce the projected benefits paid out considerably, particularly towards the latter half of the projected period;

- adjusting for the short-term pay freeze in the public sector and public service workforce reductions also reduces the projected future payouts compared to previous projections, both by size of pension benefit and the number of people expected to receive pensions; and

- offsetting these factors to some extent is an allowance made for the public service workforce to increase in the longer term, a little less than population growth (previous analysis assumed a constant public service workforce).

4.30 The allowance for a short-term reduction in the public service workforce means that the lower percentages towards the right of the chart reflect lower total payments (as a percentage of GDP) but paid to fewer people than would have been otherwise. Payments made per individual would not decrease to the same extent.

4.31 The projections are dependent on the assumptions that lie behind them and so need to be treated cautiously. The Commission has asked GAD to carry out sensitivity analyses to assess how the projections would be impacted by altering a set of key assumptions, namely productivity and real earnings growth, public service workforce growth and life expectancy. The results of this analysis can be found in Chart 4.B with further details in Annex B.

4.32 The result of varying these key assumptions is shown to increase or decrease assumed benefit payments by around 0.2 per cent of GDP by 2059-60. This is equivalent to around £7 billion in today's prices. In addition to this, the Commission estimates that if the long-term gap between RPI and CPI was lower than assumed (0.5 per cent rather than 0.75 per cent), the projected costs could be higher by around a further 0.1 per cent of GDP. This illustrates the level of uncertainty in making projections of this type. The actual outcomes could fall outside the band shown if future experience differs materially from the assumptions used in the central projection.

Chart 4.B: Projected benefit payments as a percentage of GDP – sensitivity analysis

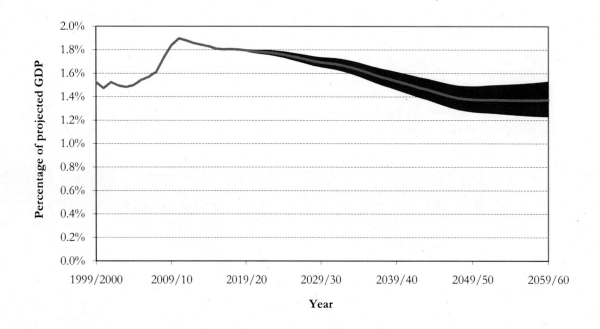

Source: GAD projections for IPSPC and IPSPC analysis.

4.33 Charts 4.A and 4.B show that the cost of public pensions is a significant element of public expenditure now and in the future. The fact that the cost may well fall in the future may be somewhat reassuring but it does not mean that there are no issues to be addressed. On the contrary, it remains important that proper account is taken of longevity risks and that public employees pay a fair share of the cost of their pensions.

Sustainability: managing the risks around cost of provision

Longevity

4.34 One of the major uncertainties in relation to pension costs relates to how long pensioners are expected to live. In this respect public service pensions are little different to any other form of pension provision. Longevity has increased dramatically over the past 50 years. Chart 4.C illustrates how life expectancies from age 60 in England have generally increased over this period for males and females.

Chart 4.C: Period life expectancies for those reaching age 60 – general population

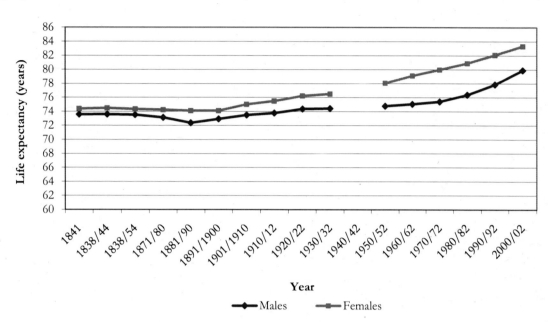

Source: Life tables 1-16, ONS

Box 4.C: Period and cohort life expectancies

When discussing life expectancies, it is important to distinguish between period and cohort life expectancies.

Period life expectancies represent the amount of time an individual is expected to live if mortality rates were equal to the experience of other individuals in that year. For example, the period life expectancy of a 60-year old in 2010 will be worked out using the actual mortality rates for age 60 in 2010, age 61 in 2010, age 62 in 2010 and so on.

In contrast, cohort life expectancies estimate an individual's probability of surviving future years allowing for possible changes in mortality rates over time. For example, the cohort life expectancy of a 60-year old in 2010 will be worked out using the actual mortality rate for age 60 in 2010, the expected mortality rate for age 61 in 2011, the expected mortality rate for age 62 in 2012 and so on.

Period life expectancies are a more objective measure as they rely on observed mortality rates. However, they do not allow for any future changes in mortality rates and so are less useful for predicting future life expectancies. Cohort life expectancies include an allowance for future changes in mortality rates and are therefore more useful for predicting future life expectancies. However, the allowance for future improvements in mortality rates does introduce a measure of subjectivity into the calculation.

Where individuals are expected to live longer over time (as has occurred historically in the UK), cohort life expectancies will give higher life expectancies than period life expectancies, all else being equal.

4.35 When scheme valuations are carried out the assumptions made about longevity are key in determining the recommended employer contribution rate. If members are living longer, then for a given retirement age pensions are paid for longer and therefore higher contributions are required to fund the higher cost.

Life expectancy in public service pension schemes

4.36 Chart 4.D shows how life expectancy assumptions for public service valuations have changed since early valuations of the teachers, NHS and civil service schemes. A female retiring from the NHS scheme aged 60 in 1956 was expected to live for a further 19.8 years. By 2004 this expectancy had increased to 28.0 years and by 2010[8] to 32.3 years. These are cohort life expectancies and therefore allow for estimated future improvements in life expectancy.

4.37 It has sometimes been suggested that public service pension schemes are underestimating life expectancies compared to the private sector. However, the evidence the Commission has does not support this. The last bar of Chart 4.D includes an estimate of average life expectancy assumptions for private sector schemes in 2008[9] (the latest figures available). There are, of course, differences in the demographic make up of public service and private sector scheme members which may lead to justified differences in assumptions.

---

8 The most recent published actuarial valuations for teachers and NHS are effective as at 2004 with new valuations expected shortly. There was a valuation of the civil service scheme in 2007 but we have used the 2003 valuation for consistency with the teachers and NHS valuations.

9 IPSPC estimates for pensioners aged 60 based on average male life expectancies from 65 presented in the Pensions Regulator's report 'Scheme funding: An analysis of recovery plans' published in November 2009. http://www.thepensionsregulator.gov.uk/docs/scheme-funding-analysis-2009.pdf.

Chart 4.D: Cohort life expectancy assumptions for current pensioners aged 60 by scheme

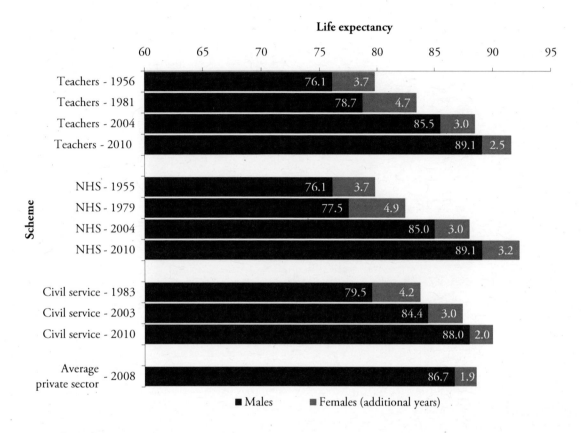

Source: IPSPC analysis of GAD valuation reports, 2009-10 resource accounts and analysis of private sector recovery plans by the Pensions Regulator, November 2009.

4.38 These increases in life expectancy have meant that current employees can expect to spend a greater proportion of their adult lives in retirement than employees when the schemes were set up. Chart 4.E compares the expected proportion of adult life spent in retirement for pensioners from the NHS Pension Scheme over the past 50 years who retired at age 60 (the earliest they could take benefits without actuarial reduction).

Chart 4.E: Assumed proportion of adult life in retirement, NHS Pension Scheme

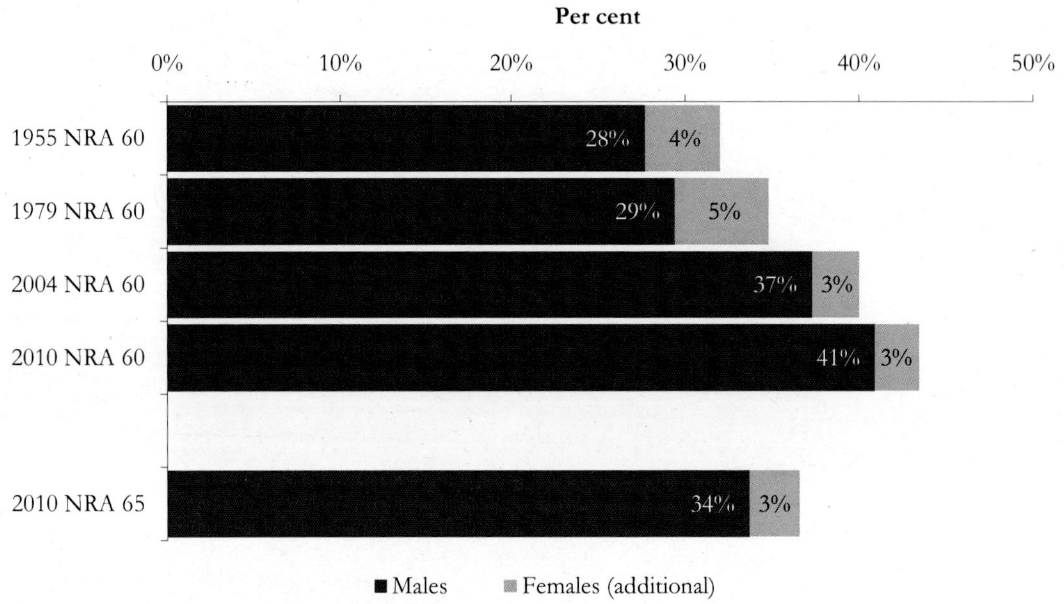

Per cent

0%	10%	20%	30%	40%	50%

1955 NRA 60 — 28% 4%

1979 NRA 60 — 29% 5%

2004 NRA 60 — 37% 3%

2010 NRA 60 — 41% 3%

2010 NRA 65 — 34% 3%

■ Males   ■ Females (additional)

Source: IPSPC analysis of GAD valuation reports.

4.39 Chart 4.E shows that current pensioners can expect to spend around 40-45 per cent of their adult lives in retirement if they retired at 60, compared with around 30 per cent for pensioners in the 1950s. This increase has been partially offset by increasing the normal retirement age to 65 for new entrants into the scheme.

Increasing cost due to increasing life expectancy assumptions

4.40 Whilst greater longevity is a positive development, the unprecedented rise in life expectancy since the schemes were set up has meant that providing public service pensions have become significantly more expensive than was anticipated.

4.41 This is illustrated in Chart 4.F by showing how the standard contribution rate for the NHS Pension Scheme calculated in 2004[10] (the date of the latest published valuation) would have changed if the 1955, 1979 and the 2010 Resource Account life expectancy assumptions had been used instead (i.e. leaving all other assumptions, including the 3.5 per cent real discount rate unchanged).

---

10 Expressed as the standard contribution rate, without allowing for deficits or surpluses.

Chart 4.F: Estimated standard contribution rates in 2004 for the NHS Pension Scheme using alternative longevity assumptions (as a proportion of salaries)

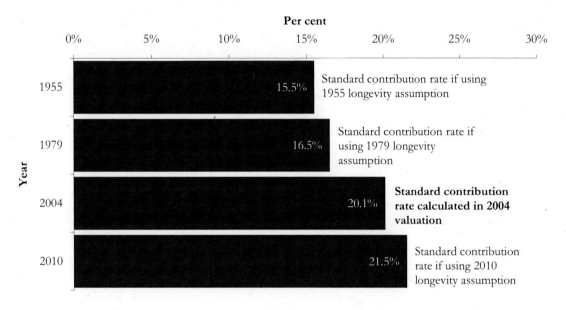

Source: IPSPC analysis using GAD valuation reports and Resource Accounts.

4.42 The cost of pensions in 2004 was a third higher than it would have been if assumptions about life expectancy were the same as those in 1955. Similar results can be calculated for the other unfunded schemes. This increase in cost has mostly been paid for by employers and taxpayers.

4.43 This analysis does not take into account the reforms to the NHS Pension Scheme since 2008. New members have a pension age of 65 instead of 60; members can take more pension as lump sum on a basis that reduces scheme costs in the long-term; employee contribution rates increased by an average of around 0.5 per cent starting in 2008; and pensions will now rise by CPI inflation rather than RPI inflation.

Uncertainty around longevity

4.44 It is generally assumed that longevity will continue to increase in the future. Increases in life expectancy have historically been recognised by producing future projections but the rate of improvements has been consistently underestimated. This is illustrated in Chart 4.G.

4.45 The chart emphasises that it is not possible to be confident about what the longevity experience will be in the future. Because of this, it is how the uncertainty is measured and managed that is important within a pension system. The implication of increasing, but uncertain, life expectancy is that schemes should have mechanisms in place to control these costs. The cap and share arrangements discussed in Chapter 2 are an example of such a mechanism. Other possibilities for such mechanisms are something the Commission will consider further in the final report.

Chart 4.G: Actual and projected period life expectancy at birth for UK males

Source: IPSPC analysis drawing on C Shaw, 2007 and ONS, 2008 population projections.

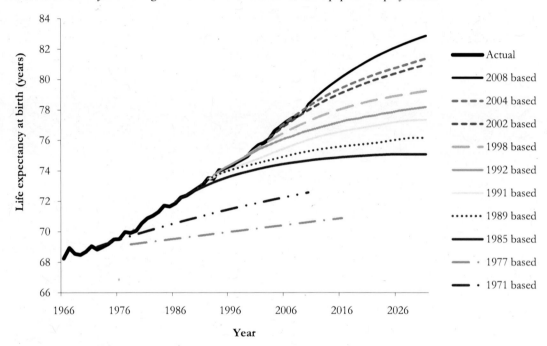

Impact of discount rates on measuring costs and contributions

4.46 The choice of discount rate has a significant effect on the measurement of the costs of public service pensions, particularly those expressed as accrued liabilities, current service costs and standard contribution rates.

Box 4.D: What is a discount rate?

Pensions are long-term commitments. An employee joining a public service pension scheme at age 25 will probably receive pension payments between 40 and 70 years in the future.

One method used to understand the cost of pension promises made to date is to calculate the present value of expected pension payments in the future using an appropriate discount rate.

To explain discount rates in more detail, let us assume that a company promises an individual a payment of £100 in 10 years' time. What is the cost of that promise now to the company?

The cost to the company could be considered to be the amount of money needed now in order to pay £100 to this individual in 10 year's time.

Let us assume that the company decides that it will invest in government bonds and it expects that these will give a return of 4 per cent[a] per year. The cost to the company of providing £100 in 10 year's time is therefore:

$$£100 \div 1.04^{10} = £67.56$$

Effectively, the 'discount rate' used is 4 per cent, which is equal to the expected return on government bonds.

Alternatively, the company may decide to invest in equities, where it expects a return of 8 per cent[b] per year. The cost of the company of providing £100 in 10 years' time (using a discount rate of 8 per cent) will then be:

$$£100 \div 1.08^{10} = £46.32$$

So it may appear as though the company should invest in equities. This isn't necessarily the case, because equities are more risky than government bonds and so if the company invests in equities there is an increased chance that the £46.32 they invest now may be less than £100 in 10 years time and they may need to make up the difference.

The concept of a discount rate becomes more difficult with unfunded public service pensions as there are no assets to back the pension promises.

A final point to note is that the individual may put an entirely different value on the £100 which may reflect how much they value money now rather than later, how much they think £100 will buy in 10 years and how certain they think they are to get the £100. The Commission has not attempted to quantify this in any analysis.

a 4 per cent nominal, so not adjusted for prices.

b 8 per cent nominal, so not adjusted for prices.

4.47 The appropriate discount rate to use is dependent on what the resulting calculations will be used for. Within public service pensions, the Government uses discount rates for two main purposes: financial reporting (in Resource Accounts, which are annual accounting statements constructed in a similar manner to those of private sector companies) and setting employer contribution rates (through actuarial valuations carried out every 3 to 4 years).

4.48 Resource Accounting uses a discount rate based on AA corporate bond yields, broadly in line with the private sector. This chapter has noted the volatility in cost calculations that result from using AA corporate bond yields as a discount rate and the limitations of the resulting figures, but also that it aids comparability with the private sector. The Commission has no further comment on this at this time.

4.49 However, the Commission considers that getting the discount rate right in setting contribution rates is key to assessing the cost of benefits being provided in each of the schemes, ensuring those costs are properly allowed for in workforce planning and budgeting and enabling those costs to be appropriately divided between employer and employee and facilitating proper comparisons between remuneration in the public and private sectors

4.50 Actuarial valuations assess the cost of benefits being earned in the schemes by calculating the standard contribution rate. They also assess the overall current contribution rate that should be paid after taking account of any notional surpluses and deficits from under or over estimates of costs at previous valuations and set the scene for determining how the overall rate should be allocated between employer and employee.

The current discount rate

4.51 The rate used for actuarial valuations of unfunded schemes was set at a fixed level of 3.5 per cent above RPI inflation in the late 1990s and has not changed since. The rate was designed to be a stable, notional rate that is not referenced to a specific set of investments. When it was set at 3.5 per cent this was in line with the Government's 'social time preference rate' (see Box 4.E) and a view taken at the time on what the very long-term cost of Government borrowing might be.

4.52 Using this discount rate reflects the unfunded nature of public service pension schemes by treating the schemes as inter-temporal transfers within the public sector, in line with other public investment projects. This approach has been questioned in two ways: firstly, if the time-preference approach is considered appropriate, whether 3.5 per cent is the right rate to use for public service pensions; and, secondly, whether a time-preference approach is appropriate at all.

Box 4.E: Social Time Preference Rate

The Social Time Preference Rate (STPR) is set out in The Green Book, HM Treasury's guidance for the appraisal and evaluation of Government policies, programmes and projects. It is defined as the value society places on current consumption as opposed to future consumption.

The rate, r, is made up of 2 components:

1) The rate at which individuals discount future consumption over present consumption, assuming no change in per capita consumption is expected

This is represented by $\delta + L$ where:

δ: Pure time preference (reflecting preference for consumption now rather than later with the same level of resources available)

L: Catastrophe risk (the likelihood that all returns from projects will be radically and unpredictably altered)

2) If per capita consumption is expected to grow over time, an element reflecting the fact that future consumption will be plentiful relative to the current position and therefore have lower marginal utility

This is represented by $g * \mu$ where

g: Growth in per capita consumption

m: The elasticity of marginal utility of consumption

The current rate is calculated using d = 0.5 per cent, L = 1.0 per cent, g = 2 per cent and m = 1.

i.e. r = 0.5 per cent + 1.0 per cent + 2.0 per cent * 1 = 3.5 per cent

Source and further information: The Green Book, HM Treasury..

An appropriate social time preference rate for public service pensions

4.53 It may be appropriate to use a social time preference rate on the basis that it represents the alternative use of funding that is used to pay for public service pensions. It also has the benefit of being stable over time. However, the elements that make up 3.5 per cent may not be appropriate for public service pensions. For example, if equal consideration is given to different generations, then one might argue the pure time preference should be set at zero. Similarly, it is debatable if the concept of catastrophe risk can be applied to public service pensions in the same way as it is used to value public investment projects.

4.54 As an example, adjustments to the social time preference rate were made in Lord Stern's Review[11] on the Economics of climate change to reflect the specific nature of that analysis.

4.55 In addition, the discount rate could potentially be adjusted to allow for the long-term nature of pension liabilities. The Green Book states that where appraisals are materially dependent on discounting effects, a lower discount rate could be used for the longer term: 3.5 per cent is given for the period of 0-30 years, with 3.0 per cent for 31-75 years.

A different approach to the discount rate

4.56 Alternative suggestions for an appropriate discount rate have been made. The Commission consider three options here:

- an approach consistent with private sector and local government funding;

- a rate based on the yields on government bonds; and

- a rate in line with expected GDP growth.

Private sector and local government funding

4.57 Private sector funding is prescribed by Scheme Funding legislation. The approach to setting discount rates generally considers the strength of the employer covenant,[12] the assets held by the scheme to fund the liabilities and the market yield on government bonds. Similar regulations control the funding valuations of Local Government Pension Schemes. Of course, unfunded schemes do not hold assets. However, it could be argued that a consistent approach would be to consider a private employer of the strongest covenant or a Local Government employer. Using the most recent data published by the Pensions Regulator[13] and analysis of the 31 March 2007 English LGPS valuations, the Commission estimates this could be in the region of 2.5 to 3.0 per cent above RPI inflation.

---

11 Stern Review on the Economics of Climate Change. Pure time preference was set at 0 per cent, catastrophe risk at 0.1 per cent, growth in per capita world production at 1.3 per cent and elasticity of marginal utility of consumption at 1. The rate used was therefore 1.4 per cent.

12 The ability and willingness of the employer to support the pension scheme in the long-term.

13 http://www.thepensionsregulator.gov.uk/docs/scheme-funding-analysis-2009.pdf, Table 4.1 and Figure 4.1. These show that between September 2005 and September 2008 (the latest data available), average discount rates used by all private sector schemes for Scheme Funding purposes were between 2 per cent and 2.5 per cent above RPI inflation, with a range of around 1.5 per cent. Given that the Scheme Funding legislation allows schemes with a stronger sponsoring employer to use higher discount rates (as they are more likely to be able to fund any deficit that arises if investments do not perform at this level), it appears reasonable to assume that the average discount rate currently being used by private sector schemes sponsored by a employer with a strong covenant is likely to be in the region of 2.5 per cent to 3 per cent above RPI inflation.

Government bond yields

4.58 Some evidence received by the Commission argued that as pension contributions are being used to finance current government spending, pension liabilities should be discounted at the market rate of Government borrowing, for example the current yield on index-linked gilts, which has recently been around 0.8 per cent above RPI inflation.

4.59 There have been various criticisms of this method, including:

- it is not practical for the Government to set contribution rates using a market rate which fluctuates so much from day-to-day, since this would produce significant and artificial changes in the size of contributions required;

- current low index-linked gilt yields may reflect an undersupply of such bonds in the market, which drives yields artificially low as the price of such bonds increases;

- the price (and therefore yield) placed on gilts by the market tells us the value of these bonds to the private sector. The Government is not a buyer of gilts but a monopoly seller. The Government should expect the price of index-linked gilts to fall as more bonds are issued, which will increase the yield and the cost to the Government of future borrowing; and

- building on the arguments above, if the Government were to issue index-linked gilts to the value of the accrued liability of unfunded public service pension schemes, it is likely that the yield on index-linked gilts would rise significantly from its current level.

Expected GDP growth

4.60 The argument for a discount rate in line with GDP growth centres on the idea that pensions from unfunded schemes will be paid for out of future tax revenue by future taxpayers and so pensions should be valued by discounting at the rate at which tax revenue is expected to grow. Over the long term, tax revenues could be expected to rise broadly in line with GDP and so a reasonable proxy to the growth in tax revenues could be the expected long-term future rate of GDP growth. A discount rate based on this approach may be around 2 to 2.5 per cent above RPI inflation, based on recent forecasts.

Impact of changing the discount rate on contribution levels

4.61 Contribution rates are very sensitive to the choice of discount rate. Keeping all other assumptions unchanged, a lower discount rate results in higher contribution rates and vice versa. The Commission estimates that for unfunded schemes as a whole, the effect of reducing the discount rate by 0.5 per cent per annum could increase the calculated total contribution required by an average of about 3 per cent of pay or £3 billion to £4 billion a year.

4.62 Any increase in contributions resulting from this change would need to be fairly distributed between employees and employers (representing the taxpayers' contribution).

4.63 A change in discount rate would also affect the value placed on liabilities relating to past service as well as future service. If a change was made, Government would need to consider how best to deal with a past deficit in a manner that was fair and reasonable.

Discount rates: conclusion

4.64 Assessing the cost of any defined benefit (DB) pension scheme depends on numerous assumptions and cannot be calculated with any certainty. However, an estimate of the cost of providing for pensions must be calculated in order that the Government and both public service employers and employees are aware of the cost of benefits being accrued and contributions can be set appropriately. The right discount rate is key to this.

4.65 The Commission therefore recommend that the Government review the use of the current rate of 3.5 per cent above RPI inflation, in the context of actuarial valuations used to set employer contribution rates, preferably concluding in time to inform the Commission's final report.

4.66 This review should also consider whether future discount rates should be expressed in terms of CPI inflation rather than RPI inflation for consistency with how benefits will be increased in payment or consider a nominal rate.

The funding basis for public service pension schemes

4.67 Currently most public service pension schemes are unfunded. There has been criticism of this, for example because of concerns that:

- the accrued pension liability is very large and has been growing significantly over time, even if the actual year-on-year liability totals fluctuate up and down;

- future taxpayers and public finances might be better protected if monies were specifically set aside and invested to meet these future payments;

- if the Government had invested more significantly in the UK through pension funds this might have increased UK capital stocks and productivity; and

- lack of transparency about the division of the real cost of pensions between employer, employee and the future taxpayer is unhelpful.

4.68 However, the Commission considers that the size of the liabilities should not determine the funding structure. The UK government is unlike private sector organisations in that the State is permanent and has the power to tax to meet long-term liabilities, so funding is not required to safeguard its pension promises. Also, the benefits represented by the total accrued liability will be paid out gradually over the 21st century.

4.69 There are some fiscal management issues relating to unfunded schemes that government needs to handle carefully. For example, if pensioners were to become such a large proportion of the overall population that taxpayers could not support the level of spending on their pensions. But such demographic challenges and related annuity risks also impact on funded schemes, for example through the increasing proportion of national income that would need to be allocated through the funds to pensioners and the impact of the build up and run down of those funds on asset prices and consumption.

4.70 It is also doubtful whether increasing government taxation and borrowing to invest monies in pension funds would lead to higher economic growth. Government might have increased its contribution to savings within the UK when a pension scheme was in the initial "accumulation" phase, when numbers of members in employment greatly exceeded the number of pensioners. But scheme members and taxpayers would be paying for that saving and might have reduced voluntary savings elsewhere. When the government funded scheme was mature, as many of the public service pension schemes are, it would be a net drawer on savings not a net saver.

4.71 It is worth bearing in mind that if it were really regarded as good for national economic growth for the Government to tax and borrow much more in order to invest for the long-term, rather than leaving monies and investment decisions with businesses and individuals, such logic could be extended beyond public service pensions to State benefits and services in general.

4.72 Keeping schemes unfunded also has the advantages of avoiding:

- the significant investment management costs, which vary by class of asset but can be equivalent for active fund management to anything from 0.2 per cent of the value of the assets being managed each year to 1 per cent or more;

- the significant risks involved in investing, whether in the UK or overseas;

- government in one guise or another controlling up to a trillion pounds or more of financial assets;[14] and

- the risk of placing the funds in the hands of trustees, in a situation in which taxpayers would be exposed to the investment risk but those investing would know that, in an emergency, Government might be compelled to underwrite the funds.[15]

---

14 The most recent Government estimate of unfunded scheme accrued liabilities was £770 billion as at March 2008, as set out in the 2009 Long-term public finance report, published by H M Treasury.

15 It is sometimes suggested that special government stocks might be issued that would be held only by public service pension schemes but that would involve setting a non-market interest rate and add extra administrative costs to existing arrangements for valuing schemes and charging contributions.

4.73 Any change to funded from unfunded status would also involve significant transition costs. The contributions in respect of current employees that are used at present to help finance pensions in payment would have to be diverted to the new pension funds. Those unfunded pensions in payment would then have to be financed through extra government borrowing or taxation. That could cost £20 billion or more a year[16] for many years and the cost would only decline very gradually over the 21st century. That extra financing cost makes it very difficult, particularly at a time of fiscal consolidation, to move unfunded pensions on to a funded basis.

4.74 Given these issues the Commission believes that it is reasonable, on balance, for Government to structure their public service pension provision on a mainly unfunded basis.

4.75 However, the Final Report will consider whether there is a case in some areas for a partially funded model, for example to diversify provision and spread risk.

The Local Government Pension Scheme

4.76 As discussed in Chapter 1, the Local Government Pension Scheme (LGPS) is in a different position to the other very large public service pension schemes in that it is a funded scheme. Employers and employees pay their contributions into a fund and these contributions are invested in assets that produce investment returns. Current pensions are paid from the fund.

4.77 However, the LGPS is not subject to the same regulation as funded DB schemes in the private sector. The LGPS is not trust-based, decisions regarding fund governance and employer contribution rates are instead made by the administering authority of each LGPS fund. In addition, it is not subject to the same funding and regulatory requirements that apply to most funded schemes.

Measuring the cost of the LGPS

4.78 In common with unfunded public service pension schemes, there are a number of measures that can be used to measure the cost of the LGPS. Due to the availability of data, in particular that contained in the Audit Commission's July 2010 information paper 'Local government pensions in England',[17] the Commission focuses its analysis in this section on the 79 English LGPS funds. The Commission will consider data from all LGPS funds in the UK in reaching conclusions in its final report.

---

16 Based on total expected contribution to the central government unfunded schemes in 2010-11 of £21.2 billion (Table D1 of Public Expenditure Statistical Analysis 2010 by HM Treasury in July 2010). Contributions for police and firefighters are paid in addition.

17 www.audit-commission.gov.uk/localgov/nationalstudies/localgovpensions/Pages/Default_copy.aspx

4.79 In contrast to the unfunded public service pension schemes, cash flow (contributions received less benefits paid) is currently positive in the LGPS. In 2008-09, contributions from employers and employees for all English LGPS schemes totalled £7.3 billion, with benefits payable of £5.6 billion, a positive cash flow of £1.7 billion.[18] As funds mature and pensioners increase relative to employees, cash flow will likely turn negative, as for the unfunded public service pension schemes. The Audit Commission estimates that assuming workforce numbers stay at 2010 levels, cash flow will turn negative in 2025, or in 2016 assuming a 15 per cent per cent workforce reduction over the next 5 years.[19]

4.80 Individual employers participating in the LGPS produce accrued liability and current service cost estimates for inclusion in their accounts each year, broadly in line with private sector practice. Due to the number of employers participating in the LGPS and the fact that many of them do not share the same accounting date, it is difficult to construct an aggregate accrued liability or current service cost figure across the LGPS. In addition, many of these employers are private sector companies participating as admitted bodies in the LGPS and so these figures would overstate the public service accrued liability or current service cost.

4.81 Standard and current contribution rates are set through fund valuations carried out every 3 years. The latest completed English LGPS valuations were carried out at 31 March 2007. Current contribution rates for employers (net of employee contributions) range from 14 to 25 per cent of pay,[20] with an average of around 18 per cent of pay. On average, these current contribution rates include 5 per cent of pay to restore funding levels to 100 per cent over a period of 10-30 years from 31 March 2007.[21]

4.82 In July 2010, the Audit Commission estimated that the aggregate funding level across the English LGPS funds had fallen to around 72 per cent at 31 March 2010 compared to 84 per cent at 31 March 2007.[22]

4.83 This 12 per cent fall was mainly due to poorer than anticipated investment returns. Funds had anticipated investment returns on assets of on average around 6 per cent per year from 31 March 2007 to 31 March 2010, but actual returns over that period were estimated at 1.4 per cent per year.[23]

4.84 The fall in funding levels would have been greater but for the change in pensions indexation from RPI to CPI inflation, which the Audit Commission estimates increased funding levels at 31 March 2010 by 6 per cent.[24]

---

18 Ibid, page 19.

19 Ibid, page 19 and Figure B1 in page 9 of Technical appendices. Note these figures refer to the median cash flow of English LGPS funds in the given years, and the results for individual funds will vary.

20 There is one fund with a high contribution rate, but as a result of a deliberate choice to recover its deficit over a shorter period than other funds.

21 Ibid, pages 3 and Table 5 on page 23.

22 Ibid, page 20.

23 Ibid, page 20.

24 Ibid, page 23

4.85 On average, the Audit Commission expects this fall in funding levels at 31 March 2010 would lead to a further 5 per cent increase in employer contributions, if the increased deficit were paid over 20 years and employee contribution rates remained unchanged.[25] In practice, this analysis needs to be considered alongside the current requirements[26] for LGPS funds to have regard to stability when setting employer contribution rates.

Longevity in the LGPS

4.86 The LGPS is facing similar underlying pressures as unfunded schemes, such as significant increases in longevity in recent decades. The Audit Commission noted that between 1993 and 2008 male LGPS pensioners in England lived an extra 3.4 years and female pensioners an extra 2.2 years[27] which represent a significant increase in pension costs over the period. Most of this improvement has so far been borne by employers and taxpayers and would not be shared under cap and share, particularly given that the LGPS baseline might be set in relation to scheme costs in 2010 or later.

Discount rates in the LGPS

4.87 In calculating employer contribution rates, LGPS funds take account of the expected return on their investments in setting discount rates, rather than using the unfunded schemes' discount rate of 3.5 per cent above RPI inflation.

4.88 At 31 March 2007, discount rates above RPI inflation for individual LGPS funds ranged from 2 per cent to 4.35 per cent per annum, with an average of around 3 per cent per annum,[28] broadly in line with discount rates adopted for contribution-setting purposes for private sector schemes with a strong employer covenant.[29]

4.89 The range of discount rates is also reflected in other assumptions, which are all set on an individual fund basis, including life expectancy assumptions and the period over which any deficit arising is repaid. The Audit Commission estimated that standardising these assumptions across all funds would have affected funding and employer contribution levels at 31 March 2007 by up to 15 percentage points in each direction.[30] In practice, there are reasons why some variation in assumptions may be expected between funds to reflect different investment strategies, member age profiles and life expectancy variances across the country.

---

25 Ibid, page 23

26 In LGPS administration regulations.

27 http://www.audit-commission.gov.uk/localgov/nationalstudies/localgovpensions/Pages/Default_copy.asp, page 34 of Technical appendices

28 Ibid, page 16 of Technical appendices

29 See paragraph 4.56

30 http://www.audit-commission.gov.uk/localgov/nationalstudies/localgovpensions/Pages/Default_copy.asp, page 21 and 22

4.90 Future employee contribution rates will be set under LGPS cap and share provisions using a notional (model) fund valuation as discussed in Chapter 2. The model fund will use a discount rate of 3.5 per cent above RPI inflation in line with unfunded public service pension schemes.

The funding basis for the LGPS

4.91 As discussed above, one of the main reasons for falling funding levels within the LGPS in recent years is poorer than anticipated investment returns. One option for dealing with this risk in the current scheme would be to move away from holding funds to a completely unfunded model. This would remove investment return volatility and release cash in the short-term, in effect treating the present arrangements as a form of cash reserve that was now to be drawn down in full.

4.92 However, this might reduce employers' and funds' ability to adjust recovery periods and other assumptions, in order to limit immediate LGPS valuation pressures on employer contribution rates and Council Tax. Also, if such relaxation of funding requirements were applied to private sector admitted bodies such as contractors and charities and other non-profit making organisations, of which there may be several thousand in the LGPS, it would be equivalent to providing a new Government subsidy for the DB pensions of these private sector employers with the Government having limited control over the risk. It would also contrast with the regulatory requirements placed on other private sector employers who were offering DB schemes to employees.

Conclusion

4.93 The Commission therefore believes that the current LGPS should continue on a funded basis.

4.94 However, reviewing the LGPS's funding status will not solve some of the key underlying problems on the benefits side. In that respect, the LGPS might be regarded as equivalent in many ways to the unfunded schemes. The LGPS offers a similar set of final salary based benefits to those unfunded schemes and the membership, whether lower or higher paid, shares characteristics with memberships of those large unfunded schemes. Indeed, some local authority employers, such as in the education area, operate the LGPS alongside another public service pension scheme such as the teachers scheme. There are also overlaps between the coverage of the LGPS and schemes such as the NHS and civil service that cover similar workforces.[31]

---

31 There have been numerous examples of members moving between these schemes, on account of machinery of government changes that have altered the areas covered by the local government pension scheme.

4.95 The LGPS, in line with the unfunded schemes, will therefore need to consider longer-term structural reform of benefits and employee contribution rates to deal with such challenges.

Impact on the whole benefits and credits landscape

4.96 In examining all the issues above there is a need to be aware of the impact of reform options on the whole of the benefits and tax credits landscape. It is not appropriate to manage the sustainability of public service pension schemes by moving recipients onto state benefits.

4.97 As part of the final report the Commission will consider the impact of any changes to the ways benefits are accrued on outcomes for individuals and whether this is likely to increase costs to the benefits system.

5 Adequate and fair

Box 5.A: Summary

- Further work needs to be carried out to try and determine what are adequate levels of income for public service pensioners and what this means for long-term design of these schemes. Initial analysis suggests that public service pensions, when combined with the basic State Pension, may for those who work a full career in the public service, currently be delivering levels of income close to those recommended in Lord Turner's Pensions Commission report[1] as being 'adequate'. The Commission is seeking further views on how best it should approach the measurement of adequacy of public service pensions.

- Over half of pensions in payment are for less than £5,600 per year. But in part this reflects short periods of work and part-time working.

- The average effective benefit rate of pensions varies significantly between schemes. Those in the uniformed services are the most generous.

- Final salary schemes produce better outcomes for high flyers. Tiered contribution rates will make only a marginal impact on ensuring greater fairness in this respect.

- There will be inter-generational unfairness if costs are being passed to future taxpayers or employees, or if members of schemes before recent reforms get better deals than new joiners.

- Employer contributions have increased far more significantly over the last few decades than employee contributions in most major schemes.

- Whilst the gap between public service and private sector provision is often highlighted as an issue, this has been a result of a decline in private sector pension provision. The Government is trying to address this to some extent, through automatic enrolment and other policies.

5.1 A key outcome for public service pension schemes is that they offer a reasonable level of income in later life for public service workers. But the schemes must also be as fair as possible: between different members of the same profession; between different generations; and between employees and taxpayers in terms of the shares of costs.

---

1 Pensions: Challenges and Choices The first report of the Pensions Commission, 2004.

Adequate

Measuring adequacy

5.2 There is no universally accepted definition of adequacy, but there are two main ways of thinking about what constitutes an adequate income in retirement. Both consider a replacement rate that compares income in retirement to income prior to retirement. As a simple example, if someone earned £100 per week prior to retirement and has post retirement income of £80 per week, then their gross replacement rate would be 80 per cent.

5.3 An adequate replacement rate can be defined as either:

- allowing a household to maintain their standard of living in retirement; or

- a rate that the household deems to be adequate based on individual preferences.

5.4 The Pensions Commission, headed by Lord Turner, designed a set of benchmark replacement rates to indicate whether an individual had an adequate level of savings. These benchmark rates are set out in Table 5.A.

Table 5.A: Benchmark replacement rates set out by Lord Turner's Pensions Commission

Gross income	Benchmark gross replacement rate (%)
Less than £9,500	80
£9,500-£17,499	70
£17,500-£24,999	67
£25,000-£49,999	60
£50,000 and above	50

Source: Pensions Commission.

5.5 The benchmarks were derived by combining: economic theory, which suggests that to maximise welfare people should try and smooth their consumption over their lifetime; evidence on past achieved incomes and current replacement rates; and evidence on desired income levels in retirement.

5.6 There are a number of reasons why these replacement rates are set at less than 100 per cent, implying that households do not need as much income in retirement to maintain their standard of living:

- individuals face lower taxation in retirement (due to a combination of more generous tax allowances and not paying employee National Insurance contributions after state pension age);

- housing costs are likely to fall in retirement – for example, if households have paid off a mortgage;

- expenditure needs will be different – for example, individuals will no longer need to pay for travel to work; and

- households will no longer need to save part of their income towards a pension once they are in retirement.

5.7 The Pensions Commission benchmarks have been reasonably widely accepted. However, alternative approaches to looking at adequacy could be to use poverty thresholds as an adequate level of income, or to look at how income and expenditure needs vary across the retirement period. It may also be prudent to look at household, rather than individual income and to consider all resources available to a household in retirement (such as housing assets) rather than solely focus on income.

The level of income provided by public service pensions

5.8 There are two ways of assessing the level of income currently provided by public service pensions. Firstly, it is possible to look at the distribution of public service pensions in payment using data from pension schemes, or from survey data. Secondly, it is possible to look at the scheme rules of public service pension schemes and derive the income that someone might receive from such a scheme based on their individual characteristics. Ideally, the Commission would have liked to examine the total income of public service pensioners before and after retirement and over the course of retirement, but this has not been possible within the time available.

5.9 Chart 5.A below shows the distribution of public service pensions in payment. This shows that many pensions are for very low amounts; over half of pensions in payment are for less than £5,600 per year. There are likely to be explanations for why this is the case. Many public service pensioners may have had short or interrupted careers in public service, worked part-time, or have been on low earnings. Chart 1.E, which looks at payments from the Teachers' Pension Scheme by years of service, shows that the value of the final pension is heavily dependent upon years of service, but all the factors already mentioned earlier could lead to a small pension.

Chart 5.A: Distribution of pensions in payment by gender

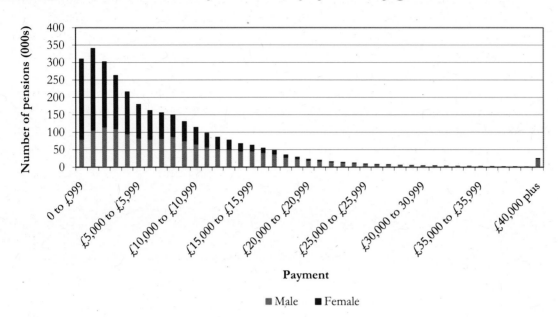

Source: IPSPC analysis of scheme data returns

Note: The largest schemes omitted from this chart are the local government scheme in Scotland and the fire and police schemes outside England and Wales. The local government scheme in England and Wales is based on pensions in payment in 2007.

5.10 People are likely to have other forms of income and not be solely reliant on the pensions shown above. All will benefit from state pension provision, some may have more than one occupational pension if they have had more than one job in their careers and some will have income from savings, investments, or other assets.

5.11 It is also possible to examine outcomes in terms of replacement rates based on scheme rules. The following example looks at the replacement rates of individuals who: accrue a full public service pension which delivers half their final salary (a typical scheme design); receive a full basic State Pension for a single person and Pension Credit if eligible; and do not receive any other income from any other source including savings, or other retirement resources (the Commission also ignores the lump sum payable from the pension scheme). In considering whether the level of retirement income is adequate, one approach is to compare these rates against the benchmark replacement rates recommended by Lord Turner's Pensions Commission, which the Commission[1] has updated approximately in line with changes in earnings since the Turner Commission carried out their analysis.

5.12 For people with full work histories, most public service pension schemes, in conjunction with the basic State Pension, appear to deliver a level of income close to, or above the benchmark levels recommended by the Turner Commission. But many people do not have complete careers in public service. If they do not accrue a full public

1 IPSPC.

service pension, then the levels of income delivered by public service pension schemes in conjunction with the basic State Pension are unlikely to reach the benchmark replacement rates outlined by the Turner Commission. This could apply especially to women who take career breaks to care for children.

5.13 Chart 5.B shows the hypothetical gross replacement rates at different income levels for people who accrue a full public service pension and people who had a five-year career break which reduced their pension amount. These can be compared against the Turner Commission's benchmark replacement rates.

Chart 5.B: Hypothetical replacement rates from public service pension

Source: Turner Commission and IPSPC calculations.

5.14 Chart 5.B suggests that replacement rates, as suggested by the Turner Commission, are being met by existing public service pension schemes, at least where people have complete careers in public service. This may well be a welcome outcome. At the lower income levels, the combination of the basic State Pension and a full public service pension produce higher replacement rates which reflects the design of the state system. But there is a good argument for saying that at these income levels, poverty levels, rather than replacement rates, should be a key consideration in designing public service pensions policy.

5.15 The extent to which public service pensions ensure that workers retire on adequate income levels is ultimately a political decision. Public service pensions could be set to deliver a level of income that allows people to reach the adequacy threshold, or just to get close to adequate levels of income in retirement, with the remainder coming from private savings or the use of assets, such as downsizing property.

5.16 The Commission recognises that additional work and analysis needs to be done in this area, including looking at household composition and income over time and is interested in receiving the widest possible range of views on this issue in advance of the final report next year. Careful thought also needs to be given to how and for which groups, adequate income levels in retirement could be delivered where people do not work full careers.

5.17 Another aspect of adequacy is whether there is a sufficient degree of certainty in terms of pension outcomes to ensure that members do not find themselves, when they retire, with too low a level of income to provide an adequate replacement income and little or no ability by then to take remedial action to boost income. Part of this is about controlling risks that are present in pensions saving and ensuring that different risks are appropriately and fairly shared between different scheme members and taxpayers.

Fair

Fairness between public service pension schemes

5.18 Factors such as the age at which benefits can be taken, the accrual rate and the level of employee contributions will all affect the value of the pension scheme to employees. A concise way to compare the generosity of schemes is to look at the average effective employee benefit rate, a concept the Commission explains in Box 5.B.

Box 5.B: Measuring the value of pensions to scheme members

To measure the value of pension benefits to scheme members the Pensions Policy Institute have modelled the 'effective employee benefit rates' of different schemes for different members. This concept tries to reflect the average value of the benefits of the pension to an individual as a proportion of their salary by taking account of the features of the scheme such as the accrual rate, the Normal Pension Age and any other benefits offered by the scheme.

These rates show the average additional value of the pension to an individual. Since they are averages, actual rates will vary significantly across individuals, depending on factors such as age, scheme rules etc. Employee contributions are deducted so that the effective benefit rates only include the part of the benefits funded by the employer.

For example, if scheme A has an average effective benefit rate of 20 per cent of salary and scheme B has an average effective benefit rate of 10 per cent, then members of scheme A are receiving benefits worth 10 per cent of salary more than those from scheme B.

To derive the numbers below, assumptions have to be made about the discount rate. In this analysis the PPI use the yield on AA corporate bond yields. A different discount rate would result in different estimates of the value of benefits, but here the Commission are interested in the differences between the value of the different public service pension schemes and how the value of public service pension schemes compare to those in the private sector.

5.19 Analysis conducted by the Pensions Policy Institute (PPI) shows that average effective benefit rates vary substantially between public service pension schemes (Chart 5.C). The reformed NHS, principal civil service and teachers schemes have average effective benefit rates of approximately 17 per cent of salary, close to the level of an average private sector defined benefit scheme (although as shown in Chapter 1 few of these remain open). The armed forces scheme is worth 32 per cent of salary, the police close to 23 per cent and the fire service around 20 per cent.[2]

5.20 Many of these differences are due to lower retirement ages and faster accrual in the uniformed services. Since the rates are net of employee contributions, the level of employee contributions is also important and the higher rate for the armed forces scheme in part reflects the fact that this scheme is non-contributory.

Chart 5.C: Average effective employee benefit rates for reformed public service pension schemes new entrants

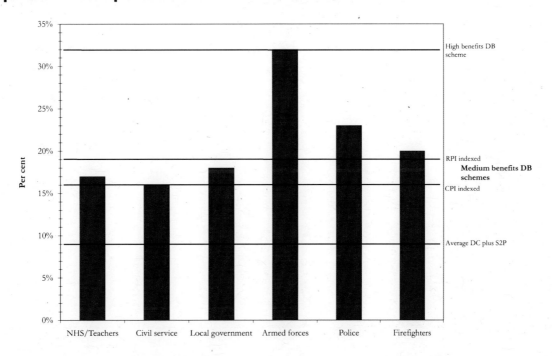

Source: PPI analysis for IPSPC.

Note: This analysis takes into account the move to CPI indexation of benefits.

5.21 There is also the issue as to fairness between what is offered by schemes. Different schemes provide different levels of benefit sometimes for people doing similar jobs, even for the same employer. For instance, school teachers in England and Wales are usually members of the Teachers' Pension Scheme, while teaching assistants are usually members of the LGPS.

---

2 Note that this data is for the post-reform public service pension schemes – the PPI estimates for pre-reform schemes are in Chart 5.F.

5.22 However many of the differences in the level of benefits delivered by schemes have arisen because of historic negotiations and developments, in particular on the extent to which pensions have been allowed for when setting pay. For example, when setting military pay rates, the Armed Forces Pay Review Body includes the value of the military pension when considering pay comparability with civilians.

Fairness between the public and private sectors

5.23 The decline in private sector defined benefit schemes and occupational pensions in general, means that the gap between private and public sector pension provision now looks much larger than it did only a decade ago. Analysis from the Institute for Fiscal Studies (based on similar methodology to that used by the Pensions Policy Insitute)[3] reproduced in Chart 5.D shows that the mean value of pension accrual in the public sector increased from 2001 to 2005, from a relatively high level, while it fell even further in the private sector.

Chart 5.D: Mean value of total benefits as a percentage of pay across all employees

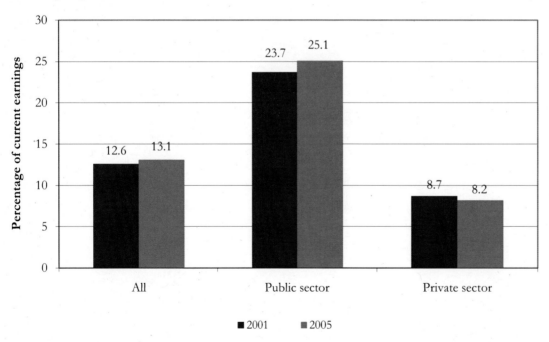

Source: Occupational pension value in the public and private sectors, Crawford, Emmerson and Tetlow (IFS).

5.24 The fall in the private sector is entirely due to a composition effect, rather than a reduction in generosity of particular schemes in the private sector. This composition effect is as a result of falling membership of more generous DB schemes in the private sector; an increase in membership amongst less generous DC schemes; and an overall fall in

---

3 The IFS analysis is based upon pre-reform schemes, does not include the recent change to CPI indexation and is gross of employee contributions.

membership of pension schemes in the private sector. Around 85 per cent of public sector employees have some form of employer sponsored pension provision compared to only 35 per cent in the private sector.[4]

5.25 However, as Chart 5.C shows, where DB schemes are still open in the private sector they provide similar levels of benefits to the reformed public service pension schemes. A medium generosity DB scheme in the private sector, which is indexed by CPI, will be slightly less generous than the NHS, teachers and local government schemes and slightly more generous if it is uprated by RPI. However, the main public service pension schemes are at least twice as generous as a typical private sector DC scheme plus any additional State Pension that someone has accrued.

5.26 On contributions to DB schemes, there is no consistent difference between the public and private sectors. A higher proportion of employees in the private sector who are members of DB schemes do not pay contributions to the scheme than in the public sector (14 per cent of employees compared to 3 per cent), or pay contributions of less than 5 per cent of pay (34 per cent of employees compared to 21 per cent). However, more employees also pay contributions of over 7 per cent of pay in the private than in the public sector (24 per cent of employees compared to 11 per cent).[5]

5.27 The real issue, though, is the disparity of provision discussed above: the widening gap between public and private sector provision in terms of coverage and that where a pension is provided in the private sector it is more likely to be a DC pension that currently tend to receive lower contributions; and therefore realise lower incomes in retirement than DB provision.

5.28 There is a fairly wide consensus that there is significant under-saving for retirement amongst large parts of the UK population. The Commission therefore supports the decision of the new Government that it will work to support automatic enrolment of employees into pension schemes and encourage companies to offer high-quality pensions to all employees.[6]

5.29 Although the Commission should be concerned about the growing divergence in pension provision across the public and private sectors, the Commission is anxious to ensure that public service pensioners achieve an adequate income in later life. However, the Commission needs to acknowledge that the difference in pension provision between the two sectors can cause particular difficulties in delivering greater plurality of public services and in achieving greater labour mobility between the two sectors. This issue is considered further in Chapter 6.

---

4 Annual Survey of Household Earnings, 2009.
5 Ibid.
6 The Coalition: Our programme for government, Cabinet Office, 2010.

Fairness between public service pension scheme members

5.30 A benchmark for fairness within a scheme could be that effective benefits from scheme membership, net of employee contributions, are roughly equal as a proportion of salary (at least over the whole of someone's career – since effective benefit rates will vary with age). So if the effective employee benefit rate in the NHS scheme is 20 per cent of salary, it might be that this should be the case for all scheme members, not 30 per cent for some scheme members and 10 per cent for others. In some circumstances, there might be reasons to depart from this benchmark, for instance for reasons of recruitment and retention of specific skills or experience, or to provide greater benefits to the disadvantaged although there are risks to using pension design for these purposes. The Commission will look further at how benefits are distributed between members including how they vary by income level and the degree to which the benefits of the low paid are lower as a share of income than those of the high paid. One of the major drivers for the variation in benefit rates between scheme members is career and therefore, income path, which is discussed later.

High and low flyers

5.31 Final salary schemes are often criticised on the basis that high flyers (those people who receive late promotions or large increases in salaries) receive far higher effective pension benefits than those who have few or no salary increases. Final salary schemes can reinforce lifetime income inequality between members, since in addition to higher salaries during working life, they can receive a pension that is a higher proportion of pension contributions than low flyers. High flyers can receive almost twice as much in pension payments per pound of employee contribution than do low flyers.[7] In addition, evidence on life expectancy suggests that high flyers can expect to live for longer and therefore receive pension payments over a longer period.

> ### Box 5.C: How final salary schemes can benefit high flyers
>
> Consider two employees who work for forty years in a scheme that provides a pension of 1/80th of final salary per year of service (a typical structure for most active members of schemes). Alice is a high flyer, whose real salary starts at £10,000 per annum and who is promoted every five years (receiving a salary increase of £5,000) to end at £50,000 per annum. Bob is a low flyer, whose real salary remains at £10,000 per annum. Alice's pension will be £25,000 per annum, Bob's £5,000 per annum. This difference is to be expected – Alice had a more successful career. But Alice's pension is worth over 90 per cent of her average salary over her career, while Bob's pension is just half of his average salary. This is due to the final salary structure, as a result of which a late career promotion increases the impact of all past service on pension receipts.

5.32 The Commission has looked at data from a large Local Government Pension Fund to investigate the connection between pension benefits and lifetime employee contributions split by final salary.

---

7 'Should Defined Benefit Pension Schemes be Career Average or Final Salary', Sutcliffe, C., ICMA Centre Discussion Papers in Finance, DP 2007-6, 2007.

5.33 This shows that each unit of contribution is buying a smaller level of pension benefit amongst pensioners who retired with a smaller final salary. For those earning below £14,000, £100 of contributions would 'buy' a pension benefit of £42 per year. For those earning over £20,000 it would buy £52, which is nearly 25 per cent more. Therefore the data seems to support the theory that high flyers are getting a better deal from final salary schemes than low flyers.

5.34 The Local Government Pension Scheme is one of the few public service pension schemes that has tiered contributions (those on lower incomes pay a smaller percentage contribution) for a significant period of time, which make the results above even more striking.

5.35 The NHS has also introduced tiered contributions, in which high earners pay employee contributions of 8.5 per cent of salary, low earners only 5 per cent. Chart 5.E shows the impact of tiered contributions on the effective employee benefit rate. High flyer benefits are estimated to be worth 25 per cent of average salary across the career, compared to 20 per cent for standard members.[8] In the absence of tiered contribution rates, high flyer benefits are estimated at 26 per cent of salary. Therefore tiered contribution rates in the NHS scheme appear to have reduced, but not removed, the higher effective benefit rates for high flyers.

Chart 5.E: Effect of tiered contributions on the effective employee benefit rate in the NHS scheme

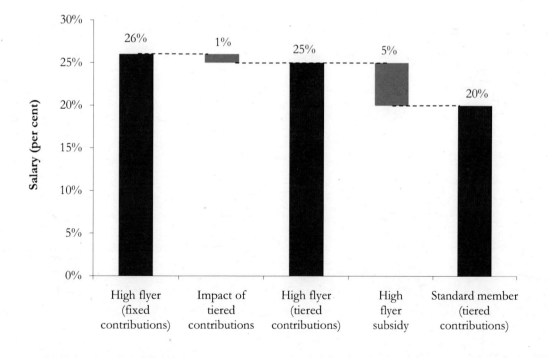

Source: PPI analysis for IPSPC.

---

8 PPI assumed that high flyers had salary progression of 1 per cent per year higher than other 'standard' members. It is assumed that there is no difference in longevity, but there is evidence that people with higher pensions live longer, which would increase further the gains to high flyers.

Distribution of costs

Between generations

5.36 Pension schemes (particularly, but not only, when they are unfunded) raise difficult issues of fairness between generations, widely discussed by economists and philosophers.[9] A reasonable benchmark for a pension scheme might be to treat different generations of pensioners equally. In a static world, this would see constant contribution and benefit rates over time. If the scheme is unfunded, taxation rates to pay for current pension payments would also be constant.

5.37 However, pension schemes need to adjust to changing circumstances in a way that does not unfairly advantage, or disadvantage, one generation. The most important change over the last few decades is the increase in longevity: in the early 1970s, the life expectancy of 60 year old was 18 years, now this is around 28 years.

5.38 Historically, the explicit response of public service pension schemes to these changes has been limited. In pre-reform schemes, longevity increases raised employer contributions, but employee contributions and benefits remained relatively unchanged. This is changing somewhat with the introduction of cap and share arrangements, which share the future risks of changing life expectancy between employers and employees.

5.39 There are other potential ways of controlling costs faced by the taxpayer as a result of increased longevity:

- relate indexation of pensions in payment to longevity. An unexpected increase in longevity would result in lower increases of pension in payment; and

- increase the Normal Pension Age, which could be linked to State Pension Age or be set independently based on past experience and future expectations about longevity.

5.40 Since neither of these measures were adopted widely for pre-reform scheme members the unanticipated increases in longevity produced unexpected gains for these members and consequently extra costs for future generations of taxpayers, see Chart 4.F.

5.41 Another inter-generational impact is caused by reforms to scheme rules. A firefighter who joined the service before 6 April 2006 is a member of a much more generous pension scheme than one joining after that date. His normal pension age is at most 55, rather than 60 and the accrual of pension benefits will become much more rapid once he has twenty years of service. The reforms to the civil service scheme have also been substantial, mainly driven by the change to CPI as the measure of indexation, which has a significant effect on career average schemes.

---

9 For example, Kenneth Howse, Updating the debate on inter-generational fairness in pension reform, (www.ageing. ox.ac.uk/files/workingpaper_107.pdf) and Barrell and Weale, Fiscal Policy, Fairness Between Generations and National Saving discuss some of the issues in more detail.

5.42 The change in other schemes is in general less dramatic, but still substantial. The Pensions Policy Institute estimates that employee benefits across the seven main schemes have fallen from about 20 per cent to 18 per cent of salary, see Chart 5.F. Of course, this is not just an inter-generational issue. Two workers of the same age who are doing the same job could nonetheless have significantly different pension rights.[10] But in general the Commission would expect older workers to be members of the more generous schemes, younger workers to be in the less generous reformed ones.

Chart 5.F: Average effective benefit rates – existing members and new joiners

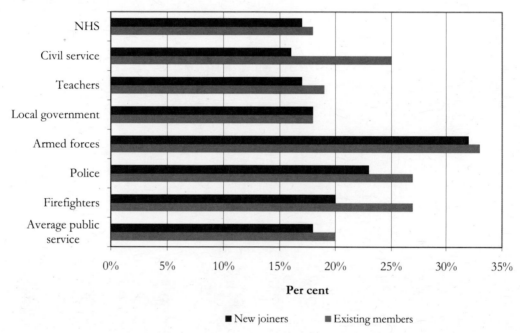

Source: PPI analysis for IPSPC

Note: This analysis includes the effect of CPI indexation.

5.43 The impact on younger public service employees should not be overplayed. Compared to their grandparents, new entrants will enjoy a longer life and the reformed schemes still compare favourably to those in the private sector, where membership of defined benefit schemes has fallen as these schemes are replaced by much less generous defined contribution schemes.

5.44 Although it may not always be possible to avoid inter-generational unfairness it should be minimised wherever possible. Key elements to this include transparency around costs and ensuring mechanisms are in place to share any change in costs, including for pre-reform scheme members.

10 Of the main schemes, only the local government scheme was reformed for all workers, the others were reformed only for new entrants.

Between the employee and the taxpayer

5.45 Taxpayers finance a proportion of public service pensions, but this is reasonable since taxpayers are also the recipients of the services that are provided by employees. However, the balance has to be right.

5.46 The split of costs between the taxpayer and the employee varies across schemes as Chart 5.G below shows. The Armed Forces Scheme is non-contributory, the judiciary can make contributions of just 1.8 to 2.4 per cent for dependants' benefits, whilst some employees in the reformed NHS scheme contribute over a third of the cost of accrual.[11] These variations are in part the result of different decisions and negotiations over pay and other elements of remuneration over the years.

Chart 5.G: Employee contributions as a proportion of the value of the accrual – pre and post reform

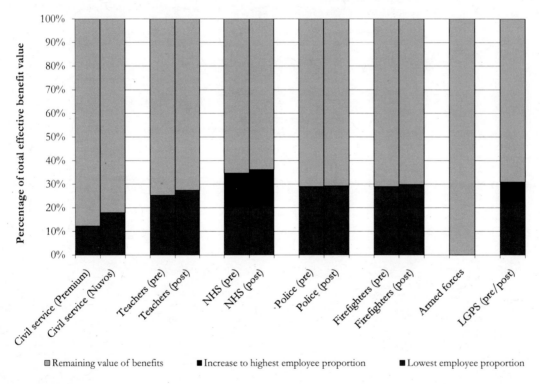

Source: IPSPC and PPI.

5.47 Although costs are important, the balance of risks between employees and taxpayers also needs to be considered. In unfunded schemes, where there are no assets there is no explicit

---

11 The analysis here uses AA corporate bond yields as a discount rate. A higher discount rate would increase the proportion of the cost paid by employees, but the impact is likely to be marginal and would not lead to employees paying the majority of the cost. The analysis has been carried out assuming CPI pension indexation in line with the Government proposals.

investment risk. However, there are risks associated with changes in longevity, so that if people live longer than expected the benefits will cost more to pay out than planned for.

5.48 The Commission outlined in the previous chapter, how increases in longevity have increased the costs of pension provisions significantly. But there have only been marginal increases in employee pension contribution rates over this period. In 1925 members of the Teachers' Pension Scheme paid 5 per cent employee contributions, which was matched by a 5 per cent contribution from the employer. Current members pay 6.4 per cent with the employer paying over twice as much at 14.1 per cent. In the NHS scheme in 1948 employees paid 5 per cent or 6 per cent with employers paying 6 per cent or 8 per cent depending on the type of worker. In 2008, employees paid between 5 per cent and 8.5 per cent based on salary and employers paid 14 per cent.

5.49 Therefore the majority of the costs are being borne by the taxpayer and the taxpayer has met most increases in cost. There may be a case for rebalancing this split of costs in the future.

6 Supporting productivity

Box 6.A: Summary

- In general, labour mobility supports an efficient labour market and enhances productivity. Pension scheme design should not be an unintended barrier to movement into, or out of, the public sector.

- Current public service pension structures appear to discourage mobility between public and private sectors through:

    - providing better benefits to those who remain within the public sector compared to those who move and thus defer their pension; and

    - providing better benefits to those who are promoted late in their career.

- Public service pensions need to be considered in the context of the total benefits package for employees. Overall, it appears that total reward, including pensions, is on average higher for public service workers than for those in the private sector, after taking account of different qualifications, ages and experience levels. There are exceptions – for instance, highly-skilled workers in London and the South East might receive lower pay and benefits in public service. But overall public service pensions are not being exploited as efficiently and effectively as they could be in attracting and keeping public service employees. Consequently current pension schemes do not appear to offer best value for money.

- It is hard to judge the impact of pensions on recruitment, given the low level of detailed understanding of pensions. But it seems likely that pension scheme members have an understanding of the comparative worth of their public service pensions. Understanding will increase as attention focuses on the prospect of reform.

- Pensions can have an impact on the different ways in which public services are provided. Evidence to the Commission has made clear that current pension structures, combined with the requirement to provide comparable pensions ('Fair Deal'), are a barrier to non-public service providers, potentially making it more difficult to achieve efficiencies and innovation in public service delivery. While some commentators have suggested that extending access to public service pension schemes would resolve this, it does not appear to offer a long-term, sustainable solution.

- Ultimately, it is for the Government to consider carefully the best way of moving forward with Fair Deal in a way that delivers its wider objective of encouraging a broader range of public service providers while remaining consistent with good employment practices. For its part, the Commission will focus in its final report on addressing the issue of how long-term structural reform to public service pensions can support greater labour market mobility and improved productivity in a way that conforms to the general principles outlined in Chapter 3.

6.1 To support productivity, public service pension scheme design should be consistent with an efficient labour market for employees. The taxpayer can then be confident that public services are delivering value for money. In general, scheme design should avoid unintended barriers to the movement of employees between sectors. This needs to be viewed in the context of the whole remuneration package, and whether the schemes support the recruitment and retention of the right people in the right jobs in a cost-effective way. In particular, scheme structure should not be an unreasonable barrier to the outsourcing and mutualisation of public services that could drive greater productivity and efficiency.

Supports labour mobility

Movement between sectors

6.2 In general, labour mobility supports an efficient labour market and enhances productivity. Pension scheme design should not be an unintended barrier to movement into, or out of, the public sector. There may be profession-specific reasons for discouraging mobility in order to aid retention. Where that is the case the trade-offs need to be explicit, clear and offer good value for money.

6.3 There are three key design features of public service pension schemes that can undermine mobility:

- vesting periods – how long an employee must stay in a job before he or she qualifies for a deferred pension benefit;

- treatment of early leavers – the extent to which those who leave public service before retirement face a penalty; and

- final salary structure – the benefit of staying on for employees who expect further promotion.

6.4 In some countries, very long service is required before a public service employee becomes eligible for pension benefits – for instance, Austria, France and Spain require 15 years' service, with early leavers having only limited rights of pension transfer.[1] But the vesting period in UK public service pension schemes is a maximum of two years, and pension rights can be transferred to other schemes after only three months' service. So in the UK this is unlikely to have a major impact on labour market flexibility.

---

1 Civil Service Pension Schemes around the World, Robert Palacios and Edward Whitehouse, World Bank SP Discussion Paper no.0602, May 2006.

6.5 The treatment of early leavers could be more significant. Moving to a job elsewhere in the public sector can be relatively straightforward, due to the Public Sector Transfer Club.[2] But problems can arise for employees who wish to move to the private sector. In most public service pension schemes, an employee's pension is based on his or her final salary when leaving public service or retiring.[3] For an early leaver who does not take a pension transfer, the pension rights accrued are then increased in line with inflation until the Normal Pension Age is reached. But had they stayed in public service the link to final salary means that those pension rights would be expected to increase in line with earnings. Since earnings tend to rise more quickly than prices over the long term, this implies that a stayer would expect to receive a higher pension for each year of pensionable service than a leaver on the same pay who takes a preserved pension, even if they have identical earnings profiles.

6.6 Some public service pension schemes provide more valuable pension rights to stayers than to early leavers. For instance, the most recent police and armed forces schemes apply Normal Pension Ages of 55 to those who retire in service, compared to 65 for those who leave early. Also, some pension designs have been specifically framed to produce a major retention incentive, such as the provision in the pre-2006 police scheme that allows for much faster pension accrual after 20 years of service.

6.7 Final salary schemes significantly increase the pensions of those who are promoted or receive a pensionable allowance, which can be particularly valuable when the increase comes towards the end of a career. A pay increase upgrades the pension rights accrued in previous years, with the result that someone anticipating a promotion or allowance could be reluctant to change jobs. This could be particularly relevant in the public sector, since Chart 6.C suggests that public sector employees – especially graduates – are more likely to have stable or increasing earnings through their 40s or 50s than are employees in the private sector. Box 6.A discusses the impact of these factors on the mobility of two different hypothetical employees.

---

2 The Club consists of about 120 occupational pension schemes, mostly in the public sector, but including for example private schools and trades unions. Individuals voluntarily transferring between schemes are able to take with them accrued pension rights and thus are not disadvantaged.

3 The civil service nuvos scheme and the NHS scheme for general and dental practitioners are based on career average earnings.

Box 6.B: The cost of job moves in final salary pension schemes

- Consider two public service employees, Alice and Bob. Bob, a typical employee, has salary increases of three per cent above inflation for the first twenty years of his working life. His earnings then increase with inflation until retirement.[a] It is assumed that his earnings will be the same whether he decides to stay in public service or move to the private sector, and that both his public service job and his potential private sector job offer defined benefit pension schemes of an equivalent generosity. A career move in early career could have a significant impact on Bob's final pension – if he changes job after ten years, his total pension will be worth about 94 per cent of the pension he would have received if he had stayed in public service throughout his career.[b] But if he changes job later, there will be little or no impact (as both his preserved pension and his salary increase in line with inflation).

- The effect could be much larger for Alice, a high flying employee, whose salary is assumed to increase at a rate four per cent above inflation throughout her career. If she changes job in mid career, her total pension might be little more than 70 per cent of her pension had she stayed in the public sector. As well as affecting mobility, the differential impact of final salary schemes on high and low flyers can have important implications for fairness, discussed in Chapter 5.

Chart: The pension cost of job moves for different employees

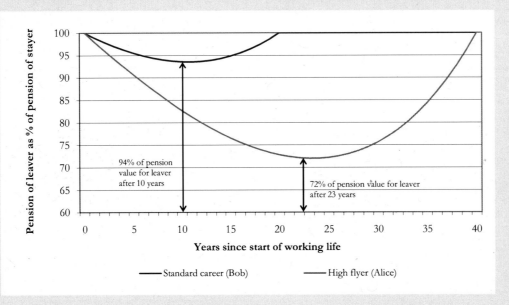

Source: IPSPC calculations.

Assumptions: Employees are members of a final salary pension scheme with an accrual rate of 1/80th for 40 years. The pension rights of early leavers are increased with inflation.

a Over the course of his career, Bob's real earnings increase by about 1.5 per cent per annum on average, similar to the growth rate of average real earnings in the UK as a whole over the last three decades.

b It is assumed that employees cannot transfer their pension entitlements across to their new pension scheme. These estimates should thus be seen as showing the maximum likely effect.

Mobility in practice

6.8 The impact of pensions on mobility is not just a theoretical possibility. Forthcoming research from the Institute for Fiscal Studies, based on a large sample of UK households, looks at the effect of differences in pension rights on an employee's choice of whether to change jobs. The study calculated the expected pension loss as the result of a job move for workers in the sample. For instance, an employee in a vested defined contribution scheme might face an expected pension loss of zero, while a high-earning employee in a generous final salary scheme might face an expected pension loss of thousands of pounds. The authors then look at which employees choose to change jobs and which choose to stay. They find that a mover between two jobs that both provide defined benefit pension plans (mostly final salary schemes) could expect an average pension loss of £500 as a result of the switch. Someone who decided not to change jobs, on the other hand, would have expected an average pension loss of £1,200 (see Chart 6.A). This suggests that the expected pension loss plays an important role in employee decision-making. Many other studies, in the UK and elsewhere, have found that membership of a final salary pension scheme tends to reduce labour mobility.[4]

Chart 6.A: Mean pension loss among stayers and movers

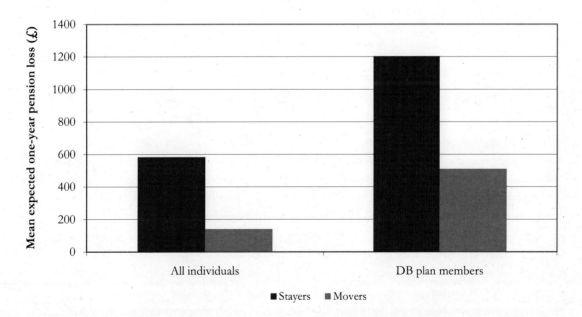

Source: Pension Rights, Choice of Pension Plan and Job Mobility in Britain, Disney, Emmerson and Tetlow, mimeo, Institute for Fiscal Studies, 2007.

Note: This shows the expected loss of pension over the next year as a result of moving job, under the assumption that all workers expect wage growth of two per cent above inflation.

---

4 Research has shown that membership of any occupational pension scheme, including a portable defined contribution scheme, is associated with somewhat lower mobility, presumably because more patient employees are more likely to choose jobs that provide a pension.

6.9 The final salary design of most public service pension schemes could thus act as an important block to labour mobility between the public and private sectors. Of course, this also implies that final salary schemes do help to retain employees. But it is not clear that they are doing so in a way that is targeted on the employees that public service employers most want to keep. Nor is this retention effect related to an employee's training; it will often be particularly important to retain those employees in whose training the employer has invested.

6.10 There is no single ideal rate of labour mobility, and there are many influences on mobility other than pension scheme design. But it is important that pension schemes do not act as an artificial impediment to an employee's choice of career. Where they do have an impact, the reasons for the design chosen should be made explicit.

The role of pensions in total reward

6.11 To be productive the public sector needs the right people with the right skills in the right location and at the right price. Remuneration is key to this. Pay is the largest part of the remuneration package, and the Commission will take account of developments resulting from Will Hutton's Review of Fair Pay in the Public Sector. Pension provision, as a sizable portion of the total remuneration package in the public sector, would be a crucial element too, if people were acting with full information and understanding.

Employee attitudes

6.12 However, people do not always make rational choices based on knowledge about their pension provision and it is very difficult to quantify the impact of pension provision on recruitment and retention. Research shows that the majority of people have limited understanding of their pension entitlement, with only five per cent saying that they had a good knowledge of pensions.[5] In addition, interest in pensions tends to be lower among younger members, with interest and knowledge increasing as retirement age approaches.

6.13 This general lack of knowledge does not necessarily equate to a lack of interest (or concern). While empirical evidence in this area is poor, it seems reasonable to assume that pensions play some role in recruitment and retention, with employees valuing their pension schemes and reacting to perceived threats to them, even if they are not aware of the details of the schemes. A recent survey of public sector workers found that 21 per cent had chosen employment in the public sector specifically for the pension and 32 per cent said they would consider a move to the private sector if their current benefits were reduced.[6]

---

5 Attitudes to Pensions: The 2006 survey, Clery, E., McKay, S., Phillips, M., and Robinson, C, Department for Work and Pensions Research Report No 434, 2007.

6 Public Sector Pensions – A Frontline Perspective, Murray, A and Wright, J., Hymans Robertson, 2009.

6.14 In addition, several submissions to the Commission from both employees and employers emphasised the importance of the pension in supporting recruitment and retention within the public services. In light of the current economic climate and the high level of media commentary on public service pensions, it appears likely that employees who are members of a public service pension scheme will be aware that their pension package is perceived as generous by wider society and better than those generally available in the private sector.

Using pay and pensions effectively

6.15 It might be expected that pensions and pay would compensate for each other in an employee's remuneration. So if two similar employees are doing similar jobs and one employee has more valuable pension rights, then the other employee should be paid more. Extending this approach to the public and private sectors, this suggests that private sector employees might be expected to receive greater take-home pay, to make up for the fact that private sector pensions are on average less valuable (see Chart 5.D).

6.16 But there is little evidence that this is so. Chart 6.B shows the median relationship between age and earnings for employees with different education levels in the public and private sectors. The earnings measures used here and later include bonus payments, but exclude pension rights, holidays and other benefits (such as private health insurance or a company car). There are some important differences between public and private sector wage profiles. For instance, highly-educated men seem to experience more rapid wage growth in the private sector, before falling back later in life. But private sector pay does not seem to be systematically higher. If anything, public sector pay seems usually to be higher for employees with low or medium education.

Chart 6.B: Median age-earnings profiles for employees in the public and private sectors

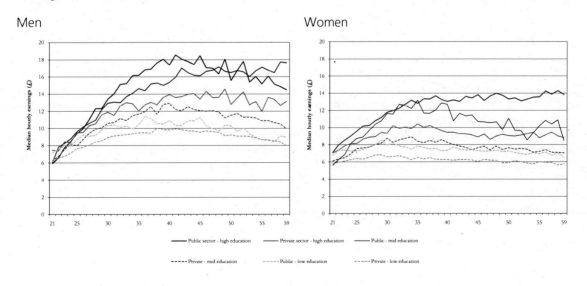

Source: 'What is a Public Sector Pension Worth?,' Disney, Emmerson and Tetlow, Economic Journal, 2009.

6.17 Of course, pay comparisons between the public and private sectors can be difficult. For a full analysis, the Commission must compare like with like, taking account of individual skills, qualifications and experience. This is not always possible, but the evidence the Commission has received shows that:

- the pay gap fluctuates over time. Public sector workers have tended to do relatively better during recessions, while private sector employees do better in booms;[7]

- overall, in the long term public sector pay differentials do not seem to depart strongly from zero.[8] There appears not to be any systematic gap between pay in the two sectors. The two-year pay freeze for public service workers announced by the Government at Budget 2010 in June could have an effect on the pay gap between public and private sector employees, but it is too early to draw any conclusions; and

- the pay gap varies between sectors and for different types of worker. In particular, research by the IFS, the Pensions Policy Institute and the Senior Salaries Review Body suggests that highly-skilled workers in the South East and London tend to earn more in the private sector. Less skilled workers, and those in other regions, typically do better in the public sector.[9] This is consistent with several studies that find that pay is relatively compressed within the public sector.[10]

6.18 The rough equality overall in pay and bonuses implies that remuneration including pensions is on average higher in the public sector once pensions are taken into account. Around 65 per cent of private sector workers lack occupational pensions (compared to around 15 per cent in the public sector). In 2008, the IFS estimated that, overall, public sector pensions add about 12 per cent of salary more to pay than do pensions in the private sector,[11] while the Office for National Statistics recently found that total reward, including pension contributions, is about 13 per cent higher in the public sector than in the private sector on average.[12]

6.19 There could be several reasons for this disparity, which the Commission plans to investigate more closely. But it does not appear that the greater benefit levels seen in public service pensions are driven by a need to make up for any imbalance in pay between

---

7 Changing public sector wage differentials in the UK, Disney and Gosling, 2008.

8 Changing public sector wage differentials in the UK, p.13, Disney and Gosling, 2008.

9 On regional differences, see Green Budget, p.226, Institute for Fiscal Studies, February 2010. On skill differences, see An assessment of the Government's reforms to public sector pensions, p.48, Pensions Policy Institute, 2008. The 2010 report of the Review Body on Senior Salaries discusses the gap between public and private sector pay at the top of the pay distribution.

10 What is a Public Sector Pension Worth? by Disney, Emmerson and Tetlow, finds that total lifetime remuneration is between three and six per cent higher for a male public sector worker with low or medium education, compared to his private sector counterpart. But remuneration is five per cent lower for a highly-educated male public sector worker.

11 Green Budget, p.172, Institute for Fiscal Studies, 2008.

12 'Total reward: pay and pension contributions in the private and public sectors', Levy, Mitchell, Guled and Coleman, Economic and Labour Market Review, September 2010. Note that this work does not take account of differing qualifications or experience levels.

the public and private sectors. This might suggest that total remuneration policies are not currently being used as efficiently and effectively as they could be to attract and keep workers.

Plurality of public service provision

6.20 In the last few decades there has been a drive towards moving services that were traditionally delivered by public service in-house providers to outside ones as a way to improve the efficiency and quality of services. The Government is examining opportunities for more private and voluntary sector involvement in service delivery.[13] It is thus likely that there will be further transfers of in-house services to new providers.

Fair Deal

6.21 At present, when employees are transferred to non-public service bodies, the organisation they move to is required to ensure that there is 'broadly comparable' pension provision for future service, through the Fair Deal provisions (see Box 6.C).[14] This arrangement has maintained the level of pension provision for those compulsorily transferred out of the public sector. However, given current public service pension structures, this can make it harder for private sector and third sector organisations to provide public services because providing a 'broadly comparable' defined benefit pension scheme can be significantly more expensive and risky for private sector organisations than for public sector employers.

13 Cabinet Office Draft Structural Reform Plan, June 2010.
14 Staff transfers in the Public Sector: Statement of Practice, Annex A, Cabinet Office, 2000.

Box 6.C: Fair Deal: the requirement for 'broadly comparable' pensions

The Fair Deal, introduced in 1999, is a non-statutory code of practice protecting the pension provisions of public sector workers that have their employment compulsorily transferred out of the public sector. If there is a compulsory transfer of staff the organisation is required to ensure that there is 'broadly comparable' pension provision for future service and that there are options for the handling of existing accrued benefits. The Fair Deal policy was introduced to generate greater workforce cooperation for public service reform. It protects public service workers from being moved to less generous pension schemes.

A scheme is 'broadly comparable' if the overall value of the benefits in the scheme (as assessed by the Government Actuary's Department) is greater than or equal to that in the current scheme. For example, since the average employer contribution rate in the civil service is 18.9 per cent of salary, a non-public service body that takes on civil service staff might be expected to make contributions at this level or higher. Furthermore, there must be no identifiable group or individual who will be materially worse off as a result of the transfer.

Given current levels of public service pension provision this code is more generous than the compulsory transfer of undertakings (TUPE) regulations set out in the 2004 Pensions Act. Broadly, these regulations require the new employer to provide matching contributions of up to six per cent of salary in a DB or DC scheme.

6.22 There are two central reasons why providing a broadly comparable pension scheme can be difficult for private sector or third sector organisations. First cost, the public service and the private sector use different bases for calculating accruing pension liabilities and the contributions required to pay for them. Employer contributions in unfunded public service pension schemes are calculated using a real discount rate of 3.5 per cent, which may be too high, resulting in contribution levels that could be too low. Employer contributions in the private sector are calculated on a 'prudent' basis within a framework monitored by the Pensions Regulator. This addresses the risk that pension fund assets under-perform, or that the size of pension liabilities is greater than expected. This typically leads to greater costs than in the public sector, where contributions are set taking into account the ultimate government guarantee. In particular, in the funded Local Government Pension Scheme, the guarantee allows more freedom to achieve long-term investment out-performance.

6.23 Second risk, by taking on employees with defined benefit pension rights, private sector bodies expose themselves to the investment and demographic risks discussed in Chapter 1. For larger firms, these risks might be considered manageable, although evidence submitted to the Commission indicates their concerns. But evidence also suggests that smaller firms and charities in particular feel unable to take on risks that could seriously harm their organisations if investments do badly or if longevity increases unexpectedly. As a result, they can either withdraw from the outsourcing process or purchase a pension from a third party. These pensions can involve contribution rates of about 40 per cent of salary,[15] more than double the average employer contribution in the non-uniformed public service pension schemes.

Extending access to the private and third sectors

6.24 Some external stakeholders have suggested that extending access to public service pension schemes to non-public service employees would help to reduce the disadvantages faced by private sector and third sector organisations as a result of Fair Deal.

6.25 Extension of access is already quite common in some public service pension schemes. For instance, the NHS and teachers pension schemes have, for historic reasons, long had many private sector employees. In the case of the NHS, this is to cover General Practitioners working as private sector practices. In the teachers schemes, it is principally to cover teachers in independent schools. The Local Government Pension Scheme has for the last decade offered admitted body status to facilitate pension arrangements for local authority workforces transferred to private sector contractors. In 2007 there were around 2,500 admitted bodies in the scheme, in addition to the 500 principal local authority employers. These admitted bodies employ about seven per cent of LGPS members.

6.26 However, there are important arguments against widening the current provisions. Doing so would involve the Government bearing additional risks arising from pension liabilities accrued in the private sector. But the Government would have little control over the liabilities being accrued, since it would not set the wages of these employees.

6.27 Some of these risks can be managed. The Teachers' Pension Scheme requires indemnities from third party financial institutions as a condition of new admission for independent schools and its rules control pensionable pay increases in the final years. But such risks cannot be completely removed, and evidence to the Commission suggests many organisations cannot provide such indemnities.

6.28 Moreover, extending access might not provide a viable solution for some private sector and third sector organisations. Evidence submitted to the Commission stated that smaller organisations are struggling with the exit charges levied by some parts of the Local Government Pension Scheme when contracts end. They can run the risk of becoming technically insolvent as they are required to recover any deficits under a shorter timescale than that allowed to public service local government employers.

Future prospects

6.29 These issues mean that extending access to public service pension schemes is probably not the solution to the issues that Fair Deal currently creates. It is clear that structural

---

15 This is based on the cost of the Prudential Platinum Pension, a scheme considered broadly comparable to those for NHS, local government and civil service employees.

reform of public service pensions could be part of a solution if reform creates a more level playing field with the private sector. The Commission's final report will deal with long-term structural reforms.

6.30 Ultimately, it is for the Government to consider carefully the best way of moving forward with Fair Deal in a way that delivers its wider objective of encouraging a broader range of public service providers while remaining consistent with good employment practices. For its part, the Commission will focus in its final report on addressing the issue of how long-term structural reform to public service pensions can support greater labour market mobility and improved productivity in a way that conforms to the general principles outlined in Chapter 3.

7 Transparent and simple

Box 7.A: Summary

- The debate around public service pensions is hampered by a lack of consensus on what are the key facts and figures and a lack of transparency of the relevant data. This report seeks to provide as comprehensive a picture as possible in order to supply the basis for well informed debate. For the final report the Commission would like to consider ways in which Government publication of figures can be improved, in content and timing, to aid transparency and whether there is a case for greater independent scrutiny, including regular independent reviews of public service pension provision.

- Public service employees need a good understanding of their pension; the choices they can make and the trade-offs involved; the implications for their income during their working life and post-retirement. Any reform must avoid the complexity that prevents such understanding and should be combined with excellent ongoing communication.

- The Commission is interested in investigating further the governance of public service pension schemes and the legal framework. While responsibilities will differ from those in private sector schemes, especially for the unfunded schemes, there is a case to consider whether responsibilities could be clearer thus aiding transparency and sustainability.

- Any public service pension system should seek to maximise value for money in administration. The Commission will consider whether there are changes that could reduce current administration costs, assess the impact of reform on future administration costs and will consider ways to implement change that will ensure value for money.

7.1 Transparency and simplicity are important concepts in the discussion of public service pension schemes. As has been shown in earlier chapters, there is a lot of confusion over public service pensions: their worth and how this is measured. The Commission has tried to bring some clarity to this debate so that any conclusions the Commission draw will be and can be seen to be, supported by the evidence.

Establishing and publishing the facts

7.2 Current discussions about public service pensions use a wide range of statistics and 'facts', many of which are contested. This makes it difficult to hold a meaningful debate on the topic. One of the aims of this report is to build agreement around the facts and figures surrounding the pensions environment and to build a consensus about which of these are important, while challenging some of the current myths in circulation.

7.3 It is also important to ensure that more comprehensive information about pension costs and memberships across public service pension schemes as a whole is published regularly and frequently and is readily accessible to the general public and Parliament, as well as to Government. There has been a considerable increase in the availability of such information in the last decade, for example, with the publication of pension scheme accounts and government projections of pension costs. However, some of this is not at present published to a regular annual timetable, for example, some of the consolidated information about accrued pension liabilities for unfunded pension schemes.

7.4 There are also issues about the different definitions used when presenting figures for different purposes. This will usually reflect the wider context in which these pension figures are being set, such as, for example, central government spending, which will exclude most pension costs relating to schemes run by local authorities. However, it is also important to bring together information about the overall position on schemes run by central and local government and unfunded and funded schemes, in a way that sets out those figures and explains the differences in their treatment.

7.5 The information available about individual schemes, or categories of scheme, could also be improved. For example, there are not the same annual consolidated overall assessments for the LGPS schemes as are provided for the biggest unfunded schemes. The overall position in England and Wales is obscured by the structure of 89 separate funds that produce their own accounts and commission their own valuation reports covering the many thousands of LGPS public and private sector employers. There is a lack of published consolidated accounts and reports that might cover the overall position across all funds and list the positions, including contribution rates, of individual employers.

7.6 It is important to have accurate up-to-date information about overall scheme costs and membership when assessing the current position and implications of possible change. Therefore, it also seems important to improve transparency by increasing the quantity and quality of published information about each scheme as a whole – whether unfunded or funded.

7.7 These issues will be considered further in the recommendations in the Commission's final report.

Clear understanding of costs and benefits

7.8 As discussed in Chapter 6 in relation to productivity, current evidence suggests that members do not have a clear understanding of the exact worth of their benefits. This does not support productivity. This needs to be addressed so that communications and pension structures enable members to appreciate the true worth of their pensions as a sizeable part of their remuneration package. Given the accepted lack of knowledge of pensions generally, including within the public sector, the Commission will be considering in its final report the role and importance of communications with employees regarding the significance and future values of their pensions within their total remuneration package.

Explaining trade-offs and offering choice

7.9 Options recommended in the final report must not be so complex that scheme members cannot be expected to understand inherent trade-offs. For example, better benefits in return for higher contributions and working longer, or vice versa.

7.10 Members will need to be able to understand the choices that might be available within new scheme structures. For example, at present members can often voluntarily decide to contribute more to provide additional benefits; this might be though extra scheme pension (added pension); extra years of pensionable service (added years) or a separate money purchase pension (additional voluntary contributions – AVCs). There might be possibilities in future for offering more choices to members around their level of contribution and scheme benefits. But the detail of such new arrangements must not be too complex to understand or administer.

7.11 It is important that in the Commission's final report any long-term structural reform options put forward for consideration should be easy to understand by the member and employer. The costs to the taxpayer of any proposals, together with the costs and benefits associated with them need to be explained clearly and transparently in a way that interested parties, the wider public and individual members can understand, including the availability of regular, comprehensive and intelligible information about pension liabilities, payments and membership.

Clarity over the legal framework and responsibility

7.12 Transparency and simplicity are important features of good governance. Pension scheme members have a right to know who is responsible for their scheme and the management of their benefits.

7.13 The governance of public service pension schemes and who is ultimately responsible for them seems to lack clarity. Whilst schemes are generally made and amended by the Secretary of State appropriate to the scheme in question, the powers conferred and their delegation can be quite complicated. Sometimes these powers are subject to consultation with, or need the agreement of, specified bodies. This gives rise to a complicated situation where decisions may be taken by many different people and of varying seniority in different schemes. Whilst in principle the Secretary of State is ultimately responsible for the scheme, it is not clear how much knowledge of the scheme and its administration they should realistically be expected to have.

7.14 This situation differs markedly from that seen in private sector occupational or personal pensions. For occupational pensions a board of trustees has more direct responsibility for the scheme, whilst in the personal pensions sector, the pension provider has responsibilities around selling and managing the arrangements they offer.

7.15 This difference in approach raises questions over whether current governance arrangements and clarity over the legal framework in public service pension schemes could and should be improved. For example, if there is a case to introduce greater independent scrutiny and regular independent reviews of public service pensions. The Commission will consider this issue in its final report.

7.16 Differences in governance also extend to the arrangements by which members are consulted about scheme developments. In some cases there are highly formalised structures. Some of these are long established, others have been updated in recent years, for example in response to the need to involve member representatives in discussions on pension reforms and cap and share in particular.

Scheme administration

7.17 The Commission understands that there is wide variation in the administration costs across schemes in the public sector, the rationale for which is not always obvious. Furthermore, these costs, at least sometimes, appear to be higher than those of similar schemes in the private sector. The Commission's final report will therefore consider pension scheme administration costs and the scope for rationalisation and cost reduction. This will include possible simplification and consolidation of functions across different schemes and units within a scheme. For example, the Commission has received evidence about the numbers of LGPS funds and how costs vary between them and possible efficiencies if that number could be reduced.

7.18 Additionally in considering options for reform the Commission will wish to take account of the cost and complexity of implementing reforms and of transitional arrangements.

Reform

Independent
Public Service
_____
Pensions Commission

8 Short-term options for reform

Box 8.A: Summary

- The current structure of public service pensions is in need of reform to meet concerns evidenced in this report, in particular on sustainability, fairness and productivity.

- However, such reform will take time to implement and to take full effect. Increased longevity, the imbalance between employer and employee contributions and the fact that total contributions may be too low if the discount rate is too high, suggests there is a case to make short-term changes, pending more fundamental redesign of schemes.

- There must be proper protection for accrued rights. Therefore changing the benefit structure is not a viable option for making short-term savings.

- There is a rationale for increasing member contributions to ensure a fairer distribution of costs between taxpayers and members. However, the Commission does not believe it would be an appropriate short-term measure to introduce member contributions for the armed forces at this time.

- It is a matter for the Government to decide the manner and level of any increases in contributions necessary.

- However, they should have regard to protecting the low paid and to the possibility of significant increases in the number of employees opting out of schemes and should consider staging increases in contributions where appropriate, to minimise this risk.

Considering the case for short-term savings

8.1 The terms of reference invite the Commission to consider the case for delivering savings on public service pensions within the spending review period. Pensions are long-term commitments and the most important outcome of the Commission's work will be establishing a roadmap for ensuring that public service pensions are well designed for the long-term.

8.2 However, in the current fiscal climate, if the evidence shows there is a need for change, there is a case for taking action that would result in savings within the spending review period. But this action must be consistent with long-term reforms intended to make public service pensions affordable, sustainable, fair and transparent in the future.

8.3 As set out in Chapter 4, improvements in longevity have affected all types of pensions provision and have increased the cost of paying public service pensions. These increases in cost have generally fallen to the taxpayer, either through increased employer contributions to schemes, or as a direct subsidy from the Exchequer when benefit payments are made. The change in the measure of indexation from RPI to CPI has offset some of these costs and should be taken into account.

8.4 In the section on the history of public service pensions the Commission reported how when many schemes were established the intention was to have a fair division of costs between the taxpayer and the employee. The Teachers' Pension Scheme set contributions at five per cent from the employer and five per cent from the employee in the 1920s. The local government and NHS schemes had similar arrangements so employees were paying around half of the cost when these schemes were initially established.

8.5 The position now is nothing like this as shown in Chapter 5. Employees in these schemes now pay somewhere between a fifth and a third of the cost of accrual.

8.6 A further complication is the extent to which the cost of pensions promises are being properly accounted for. Pension costs are split between employers and employees after the total contributions required have been calculated. This calculation involves using the discount rate that was discussed in Chapter 4. If the discount rate currently in use by schemes for making calculations about the size of contributions required is too high, then costs will be underestimated.

8.7 The Commission is asking the Government to review this rate. If they reach the conclusion that the rate is too high then total contributions to schemes will need to rise. The Commission estimates that reducing the discount rate by half a per cent, for example, could increase the total contribution rate by nearly three per cent of pensionable payroll. There is then the issue of how this increase is split between employers and employees.

8.8 Because most of the increased costs to date, driven by longevity improvements in particular, have been financed by employers in the form of increased contributions, there is an argument that employees should pay a greater share of the extra cost, as they are the principal beneficiaries of this unexpected increase in the cost of their pension.

Options for short term changes

8.9 If the Government decides to make changes in light of the analysis above, then there are two main ways of making savings from public service pensions in the short term:

- reduce the level of benefits being paid out; and/or

- increase contributions being paid by active scheme members.

Altering benefit levels

8.10 The Government has already taken steps to change how pensions in payment are indexed in line with prices, by changing the measure of movements in prices from RPI to CPI. There appears limited further scope for reducing the level of benefits being paid out in the short-term. Chart 8.A below shows the level of benefits as a proportion of GDP projected to be paid over the next 50 years by the type of member. This illustrates that the majority of benefits that will be paid out over the next spending review period are to people currently in receipt of a pension.

8.11 The terms of reference for the Commission set out that the review should protect accrued rights. The pension awards already made and often already in payment are clearly accrued rights and as such should not be affected by changes in pension structures.

8.12 Most of the other benefit payments that will be made over the spending review period are also accrued rights, but belong to current active members who will retire shortly. There is a fairly large amount of expenditure in this area because of lump sums taken at retirement. Lump sums account for around a fifth of payments to pensioners. Government could, in theory, make a saving over the spending review period, by providing incentives for people to delay taking their lump sum, or to swap it in exchange for higher ongoing pension payments. However, information provided by police, fire and NHS schemes[1] shows that people generally prefer to maximise their lump sum, so schemes would need to offer generous terms to scheme members to persuade them to give up lump sums. This would increase long-term costs at the expense of short-term savings and is unlikely to offer value for money to Government.

---

1 Evidence from scheme returns data provided to IPSPC. In the NHS scheme over half of people retiring chose to commute some of their pension to receive an even larger lump sum than the minimum amount and 80 per cent of these people commuted the maximum amount allowed.

Chart 8.A: Gross benefit expenditure by type of member

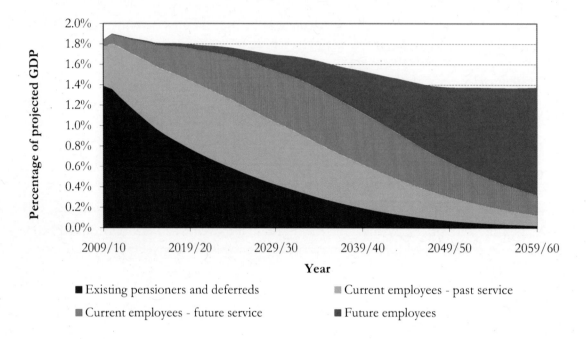

Source: GAD modelling for IPSPC.

8.13 It therefore appears that changing the benefit structure will have little or no impact within the spending review period. As part of the final report the Commission will consider changes to benefit structures to ensure that the system is fair and sustainable in the future. These are outlined in the next chapter.

Increasing employee contributions

8.14 If the Government wishes to make savings in the short-term it will be more effective to increase member contributions rather than alter the benefit structure.

8.15 To give an indication of scale, a one percentage point rise in contributions for all active public service members could raise around £1 billion per year across the unfunded schemes[2] (this is before the effect of tax relief is considered).

8.16 It is up to the Government to decide on changes to the structure and level of employee contributions. Since effective benefit levels vary considerably between different schemes, particularly between pre and post reform schemes, then changes to employee contributions could be made to reflect this. However, these differences will, to some extent, be due to historic negotiations around pensions and pay.

---

2 IPSPC calculations based on data provided by schemes.

8.17 The Commission's terms of reference set out that any case for delivering savings should be consistent with the Government's commitment to protect those on low incomes. This is important as an issue of fairness but also because of two important factors:

- it is reasonable to assume that lower paid workers are more likely to opt out of a pension scheme than higher paid workers if they face the same increase in pension contributions as a proportion of their salary. This is in no one's interests, since these people could end up with an inadequate retirement income and could fall onto means tested benefits later in life. The Government would lose revenue in the short-term since these people would no longer be paying any contributions to the scheme; and

- the Commission has shown that in final salary schemes, which still dominate the public service pension landscape, high flyers tend to do better from schemes. People with higher pensions also live for longer and so benefit from pensions for longer. This suggests that there may be a case for targeting contribution increases at high-earners, or to introduce tiered contribution levels; in a similar way that member contributions are currently tiered in the local government and NHS schemes.

8.18 To reduce the level of opt-out across the board, the Government should consider staging any increase in contributions, especially in the context of the current pay freeze. Although this might appear to reduce savings in the first few years, if it reduces opt-out levels such staging could in fact maximise extra revenue from member contributions at all income levels. In addition, the Commission does not believe that member contributions should be introduced for the armed forces at this time.

Contracting into State Second Pension

8.19 Public service pensions are currently contracted-out of the State Second Pension. This means that employers and employees pay lower levels of National Insurance, but employees are not generally entitled to receive the State Second Pension when they retire. Instead they receive the basic State Pension and their public service pension.

8.20 Reversing this arrangement and contracting public service pensions into the State Second Pension is a potential option for short-term savings, since the extra National Insurance contributions from employers and employees would be payable to Government.

8.21 However, these savings will diminish over time due to announced plans to reduce the contracting out rebate and flat rate the State Second Pension. In the long-term, in the absence of further reforms, there would be a cost to contracting in public service pensions, since extra State Second Pension paid out in the future will outweigh the short-term savings. There would also be considerable administrative issues to overcome. As such, this option does not look attractive from a value for money perspective in the long-term.

9 Long-term structural reform

Box 9.A: Summary

- The current public service pension system has been unable to respond flexibly to changes in demographics over the past few decades and the need for greater mobility between the public and other sectors.

- This system has led to disproportionate benefits for some – high flyers accruing more generous levels of benefits than low flyers – and an unfair division of costs between the employer and the employee.

- Long-term structural reform is needed as these issues cannot be dealt with through provision of traditional final salary defined benefit schemes. But neither can they be dealt with appropriately through a funded, individual account, defined contribution model for all employees, which would place a major financing burden on taxpayers, ignore the ability of Government as a large employer to manage certain types of risk and increase uncertainty of post-retirement income for scheme members, which is difficult in particular for the low paid to manage.

- An alternative scheme model that provides a fair sharing of risk between the employer and employee; and adequate pensions for members is needed.

- In the Commission's final report a range of alternative structures will be considered, drawing upon international experiences and other risk sharing models.

- This will enable the Commission to make a recommendation on a sustainable framework for a new pensions deal for the public service.

9.1 Given the evidence presented in this report, there is a case for longer-term structural reform that deals with issues not dealt with effectively under the current system:

- the rising costs of benefits due in particular to increasing longevity;

- the changing periods of time spent in work and retirement and how pensions – and pension ages in particular – can respond more flexibly to these changes;

- the unequal treatment of members within the same professional group, in particular the disproportionate benefits earned by high flyers in final salary defined benefit schemes when compared to low flyers;

- the greater need to facilitate, or at least not prevent, many different ways of providing public services and mobility between public and private sectors;

- the possibilities for increasing choice over contributions and pension terms;

- the fairer sharing of costs between employees and employers and taxpayers; and

- the management of risk and uncertainty.

9.2 This range of issues cannot be tackled through provision of final salary defined benefit schemes. But neither would it be feasible or desirable to move towards a funded, individual account DC model for all public service employees. Apart from the major financing burden on the current generation of taxpayers, who would have to pay for both employer contributions and current benefit payments, this ignores the ability of Government as a large employer to pool and manage certain types of risk better than individuals. In addition, if lower paid employees were fully exposed to investment risk, this would increase uncertainty of income in retirement, which is difficult in particular for the low paid to manage. This is not desirable or necessary. Instead, the public service should aim to identify an appropriate way of sharing the uncertainties and risks inherent in pension provision between both the employee and employer.

9.3 As part of taking this work forward the Commission will be examining innovative international models. For example, Sweden manages to share risk in an unfunded model through a particular type of notional defined contribution arrangement. This gives individuals more certainty about their accruals than in traditional DC schemes, but also shares the risk of increasing longevity through calculating annuities using life expectancy factors.

9.4 In the Netherlands, their funded collective DC schemes move the onus of risk from the employer to the members, by using solvency margins and conditional indexation while targeting career average pensions.

9.5 Meanwhile, Poland and other countries may have some interesting lessons in how they have introduced top-up funded DC elements into their pension provision.

9.6 However, the Commission will not be confining itself to international lessons, but will also be examining the whole range of schemes available where the risk is not solely placed on the employer or the employee.

9.7 This will include:

- career average defined benefit schemes that include ways to share risk and give members a pension pot after each period of membership (usually a year) that is based on a percentage of the salary earned in that year. Those pots are then usually revalued ('dynamised') until the date a pension is taken by a factor related to prices or national or occupational earnings. Those individual pension pots are then added together for periods of scheme membership to produce an overall pension;

- notional DC schemes with added protections that, while not being funded, still determine the value of pensions at retirement by an assumed return on contributions and an annuity rate or rates. In theory the latter might be linked to those available in the market at retirement or at various periods of time while the person was a scheme member, but to provide reasonable certainty would have added protections such as an annuity rate wholly or partly set by the provider on the basis of their own assessment of longevity risk and the proportion of that risk to be borne by members;

- collective DC schemes where all contributions are placed into one fund that is then managed on behalf of the members. As in standard DC schemes, members' pensions will vary according to the value of the underlying investments. However, within collective DC schemes there is the option to use inter-generational sharing to smooth the effects of market conditions;

- cash balance schemes where the employer puts a notional amount into the member's pot every year, which is then guaranteed. This credit can be expressed as a percentage of salary for each year worked. If cash contributions from the employee and employer, plus investment returns, do not match the promised 'notional credit' then the employer will have to meet any shortfall. On retirement the resulting 'cash balance' can be used either to purchase an annuity or to make other arrangements for retirement;

- sequential hybrids (or nursery schemes) that are schemes with more than one section or part where a member may earn both a DB pension and DC pension during their career with an employer. Members, however, would be earning either DB or DC benefits at any one time;

- capped DB schemes, where there is a limit on the amount of salary that counts for pension purposes or on pension payments from the scheme; and

- combination hybrids, where members simultaneously earn benefits that are part DB and part DC. For example, a capped DB pension, based on earnings up to a certain level and a DC benefit on earnings above this level.

9.8 The Commission will also consider elements of to scheme design such as:

- ensuring normal pension ages are in line with latest developments in longevity;

- reviewing rules around changes to pension payments when they are taken before or after normal pension age to increase labour market flexibility;

- the implications of different indexation options for pension costs and incomes over time; and

- accrual rates in the different schemes.

9.9 In deciding what pension design or designs might be more appropriate for the future the Commission will also take account of decisions on the new framework for pensions taxation.

9.10 Likewise, when considering what pension ages might be appropriate and whether public service pensions might continue to be contracted out of the State Second Pension, the Commission will take into account any further developments in the levels of State pension benefits; the ages at which they are available; and the arrangements for contracting out of the State Second Pension.

9.11 It will be necessary to consider the case for and against greater simplicity in numbers and types of scheme and greater flexibility for individual employers to determine pension designs, as well as who should be eligible for participation in schemes.

9.12 The Commission will also be considering the extent of accrued rights, their protection and the implications for future pensions terms. The Commission is clear that protecting accrued rights does not extend as far as protecting current terms for future pension accrual.

9.13 Pension awards already made would not be changed and neither would the years of pensionable service built up so far, based on a particular pension age, that have been accrued by those still building up pension rights.

9.14 However, after giving appropriate notice and meeting requirements for consultation on changes to scheme rules and any other legal requirements needed to manage the process of reform going forward, it should be possible to make changes to pension schemes for existing members relating to their future service. But, when deciding on the timing and nature of any reforms, it will be necessary to bear in mind that some of the present benefits, such as for death and dependants, are a form of long-term insurance. That will also need to be taken into account, when making recommendations.

Implementing change

9.15 When the Commission considers options in the final report, it will need to ensure that both the transitional arrangements for moving from current to new structures and the longer-term structures result in:

- the protection of the range of accrued entitlements provided by pension schemes;

- providing an effective transition to new ways of providing for retirement pensions and protections against risk of ill health, death and redundancy; and

- the ability to practically implement reforms, taking account of the wide range and diversity of public service groups that will be affected.

9.16 That will require appropriate planning, timetabling and administrative resources, both in personnel and systems.

9.17 The recommendations that the Commission will be making to Government are intended to provide a framework for a new pensions deal for the public service. It will aim to be fair to workers, and to suit modern working practices, whilst delivering a deal that is sustainable for the future.

Annexes

Independent
Public Service
Pensions Commission

A The Commission's terms of reference

A.1 The terms of reference for the ISPSPC were published on 20 June 2010.

Terms of reference

To conduct a fundamental structural review of public service pension provision and to make recommendations to the Chancellor and Chief Secretary on pension arrangements that are sustainable and affordable in the long term, fair to both the public service workforce and the taxpayer and consistent with the fiscal challenges ahead, while protecting accrued rights.

In reaching its recommendations, the Commission is to have regard to:

- the growing disparity between public service and private sector pension provision, in the context of the overall reward package – including the impact on labour market mobility between public and private sectors and pensions as a barrier to greater plurality of provision of public services;

- the needs of public service employers in terms of recruitment and retention;

- the need to ensure that future provision is fair across the workforce;

- how risk should be shared between the taxpayer and employee;

- which organisations should have access to public service schemes;

- implementation and transitional arrangements for any recommendations; and

- wider Government policy to encourage adequate saving for retirement and longer working lives.

As part of the review, the Commission is invited to produce an interim report by the end of September 2010. This should consider the case for delivering savings on public service pensions within the spending review period – consistent with the Government's commitment to protect those on low incomes – to contribute towards the reduction of the structural deficit. The commission is invited to produce the final report in time for Budget 2011.

Scheme coverage

- For civil servants:

    - Principal Civil Service Pension Scheme

    - Principal Civil Service Pension Scheme (Northern Ireland)

- Armed Forces Pension Scheme

- For NHS employees:

    - NHS Pension Scheme

    - NHS Superannuation Scheme (Scotland)

    - Health and Personal Social Services Northern Ireland Superannuation Scheme

- For teachers:

    - Teachers' Pension Scheme (England and Wales)

    - Scottish Teachers' Superannuation Scheme

    - Northern Ireland Teachers' Superannuation Scheme

- For Local Government:

    - Local Government Pension Scheme (England and Wales)

    - Local Government Pension Scheme (Scotland)

    - Northern Ireland Local Government Pension Scheme

- Police Pension Scheme (administered locally)

- Firefighters' Pension Scheme (administered locally)

- United Kingdom Atomic Energy Authority Pension Schemes

- Judicial Pensions Scheme

- Department for international Development – Overseas Superannuation Scheme

- Research Councils' Pension Schemes

In addition to the schemes mentioned above, there are a number of smaller schemes and many established to cover only one senior appointment which do not specifically need to form part of the review but which will be required to act on the recommendations.

B # Comparison of the different public service pension schemes

Table B.1 is designed to provide a general overview of the main (larger) public service pension schemes. It is acknowledged that there are a number of complex rules which affect scheme membership and that some members may be entitled to different terms than those outlined here.

Table B.1: Overview of the main public service pension schemes

Scheme	Name	Normal Pension Age	Min Pension Age	Members Contribution Rate	Employer Contribution Rate	Pension Basis	Accrual Rate	Lump Sum	Status
Principal Civil Service Pension Scheme	Classic (pre October 2002)	60	55 (50 prior to Apr 06)	1.5%	18.9%[1]	Final Salary	1/80	3 x annual pension	Closed
	Premium	60	55 (50 prior to Apr 06)	3.5%		Final Salary	1/60	Optional in exchange for reduced pension	Closed
	Partnership	55-75[2]		0 upwards[3]	Minimum of 3%-12.5% depending on age[4]	Annuity		Optional in exchange for reduced 'pot'	Open
	Nuvos (from July 2007)	65	55	3.5%		Career Average Earnings	1/43[5]	Optional in exchange for reduced pension	Open
Armed Forces	Armed Forces Pension Scheme 1975	55	38	Nil	29.4%	Final Salary	1/69–(1/91 for years 22+)	3 x annual pension	Closed
	Armed Forces Pension Scheme 2005	55	40	Nil		Final Salary	1/70	3 x annual pension	Open
Judges[6]	Judicial Pension Scheme 1981	65	Min 5 years service	1.8 – 2.4%	32.15%	Final Salary	1/40 or 1/80	2 x annual pension	Closed
	Judicial Pension Scheme 1993	65	Min 5 years service	1.8 %		Final Salary	1/40	2.25 x annual pension	Open
Police (England and Wales)	Police Pension Scheme 1987	55	48.5 (after 30 yrs)	11%	24.2%	Final Salary	1/60 (2/60 after 20 yrs capped at 40/60)	Optional in exchange for reduced pension	Closed
	Police Pension Scheme 2006	55	55	9.5%		Final Salary	1/70 (max 35/70)	4 x annual pension	Open

Scheme								
Firefighters (England and Wales)	Firefighters' Pension Scheme 1992	55	50	11%	26.5%	Final Salary	1/60-(2/60 after 20 yrs capped at 40/60)	Optional in exchange for reduced pension	Closed
	New Firefighters' Pension Scheme 2006	60	55	8.5%	14.2%	Final Salary	1/60 capped at 45/60	Optional in exchange for reduced pension	Open
National Health Service (England and Wales)	National Health Service Pension Scheme 1995	60	50	5-8.5% dependent on pay range	14.0%	Final Salary[7]	1/80	3 x annual pension	Closed
	National Health Service Pension Scheme 2008	65	55	5-8.5% dependent on pay range		Final Salary	1/60	Optional in exchange for reduced pension	Open
Local Government Pension Scheme (England and Wales)	Local Government Pension Scheme 1997[8]	65	50 with 25 yrs service	5-6%	13.2%[9]	Final Salary	1/80	3 x annual pension	Closed
	Local Government Pension Scheme 1 April 2008	65	55	5.5-7.5%		Final salary	1/60	Optional in exchange for reduced pension	Open
Teachers (England and Wales)	Teachers' Pension Scheme Before January 2007	60	55	6.4%	14.1%	Final Salary	1/80	3 x annual pension	Closed
	Teachers' Pension Scheme 2007	65	55	6.4%		Final Salary	1/60	Optional in exchange for reduced pension	Open

Notes

1 This is a weighted average of employer rates that vary by level of pensionable pay. The average was reduced to 18.9% from April 2009.

2 No specific NPA as such – date at which this DC stakeholder pension is taken is limited only by tax rules.

3 Members do not have to contribute, but where they do the employer provides additional employer contributions that match the employees' contributions, up to a ceiling of 3% of pay.

4 The rate of minimum employer contribution varies by age from 3% below age 21 to 12.5% at age 46 and above.

5 The annual amounts of pension earned before a pension is awarded are uprated by prices, not earnings, using the same price index as used for pensions once awarded (formerly RPI, now CPI from April 2011).

6 Some Judicial Officers had different rates of accrual, minimum service requirements and minimum age before pensions could be drawn. The figures shown reflect the position of the majority.

7 Pensions for General Practitioners in the NHS Scheme are based on career average salaries.

8 The LGPS 97 was closed wef 31 March 2008 with reserved rights to benefits earned to that date. Members were automatically transferred to the new scheme on 1 April 2008.

9 As at March 2010, based on a notional national model fund valuation using 2007 data and excludes the investment surpluses and deficits on individual local authority pension funds.

C   Projection of future benefit expenditure on public service pensions

C.1 In December 2009 the Government Actuary's Department (GAD) produced projections for HM Treasury to inform the December 2009 Long-term public finance report. These projections and the assumptions underlying them[1] were discussed in the National Audit Office's March 2010 report on the cost of public service pensions.[2] These projections exclude the cost of funded schemes such as the Local Government Pension Scheme (LGPS).

C.2 The Commission asked GAD to update their analysis for a number of developments since these results were made available.

C.3 The key updates the Commission asked GAD to allow for were:

- the change in pensions indexation from RPI to CPI inflation following the Chancellor's announcement in the Budget on June 2010;

- the short-term pay freeze, and short-term public sector workforce reductions as set out in the Office of Budget Responsibility's 13 July 2010 document;[3] and

- a central public service workforce growth assumption of 0.25 per cent per annum, responding to the main criticism of the December 2009 projections in the NAO's report above, which assumed zero public service workforce growth.

RPI to CPI

C.4 The Commission asked GAD to assume that in the future pensions in payment and deferment will increase, and career average benefits will revalue, by CPI rather than RPI inflation.

C.5 In the short-term the Commission requested that GAD base CPI and RPI assumptions on the most recent forecasts produced by the Office of Budget Responsibility. These are detailed in Table C.1.

1 http://www.gad.gov.uk/Documents/Occupational%20Pensions/December_2009_Cashflow_Projections_Methodology_data_and_assumptions.pdf

2 http://www.nao.org.uk/publications/0910/public_service_pensions.aspx

3 http://budgetresponsibility.independent.gov.uk/d/general_gov_employment_forecast_130710.pdf

Table C.1: OBR forecasts for RPI and CPI inflation

Forecast	2010-11	2011-12	2012-13	2013-14	2014-15
CPI (%)	2.8	2.6	1.9	2.0	2.0
RPI (%)	4.2	3.4	3.0	3.2	3.4

Source: OBR

C.6 Beyond the OBR forecast period, the Commission asked GAD to assume that CPI would be 0.75 per cent per annum lower than RPI. This reflects long-term observed differences between RPI and CPI due to differences in how the indices are constructed (CPI uses geometric averages, RPI uses arithmetic averages), and in the constituents of the index (most significantly CPI does not include housing costs while RPI does).

C.7 A 0.75 per cent per annum difference is also consistent with the assumption HM Treasury have used for determining cash equivalent transfer values for public service pension schemes.[4]

Short-term pay freeze and reduction in public service workforce

C.8 A two-year pay freeze was announced in Budget 2010 for public service employees. The Commission has asked GAD to allow for this pay freeze in 2010-11 and 2011-12.

C.9 The Commission asked GAD to assume that public service workforce levels would be in line with the most recent OBR forecasts in the short-term. These are detailed in Table C.2.

Table C.2: OBR forecasts for public service workforce

Forecast	2010-11	2011-12	2012-13	2013-14	2014-15
General Government Employment Level (millions)	5.53	5.47	5.39	5.23	5.04

Source: OBR

Long-term public sector workforce growth

C.10 In its March 2010 report, the NAO highlighted that the December 2009 projections assumed that public service workforce levels would stay constant in the long-term while overall employment levels were forecast to grow.

C.11 The Commission asked GAD to update the constant public service workforce assumption (beyond the OBR forecast period) to a growth rate of 0.25 per cent per annum.

---

4 www.hm-treasury.gov.uk/d/publicservices.pensions_060810.pdf

C.12 This assumption is still 0.25 per cent lower than the overall employment growth rate until 2048-49, reflecting an expectation that workforce growth in public service will be below that in the private sector in the medium-term. This assumption is included in the sensitivity analyses discussed later in this Annex.

C.13 The remainder of the assumptions for the central projection were set equal to those used in the December 2009 projections. The most significant assumptions are as follows:

- real earnings growth of 2 per cent per annum in the long-term (i.e. from 2012-13 onwards);

- life expectancy in line with the Office of National Statistics (ONS) 2008-based population principal projections, with an adjustment to mortality rates of 85% to reflect experience showing that members of public service pension schemes have greater life expectancies than the general public as a whole; and

- cap and share is allowed for using the same approach as for the December 2009 projections.

C.14 GAD advised that the central benefit payment projections (expressed in constant 2008-09 RPI prices) on the assumptions are as in Chart C.1.

Chart C.1: Central projections of benefit payments and member contributions

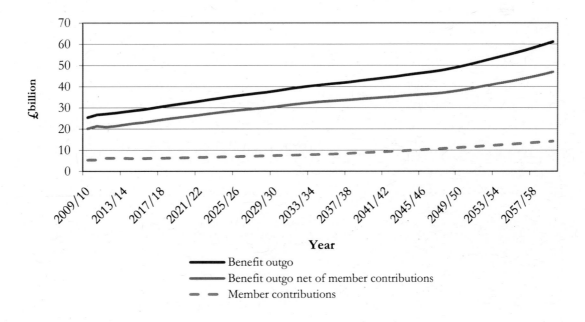

Source: GAD

C.15 Benefit payments in constant RPI terms are expected to rise from around £25 billion in 2009-10 to over £60 billion in 2059-60. Employee contributions are expected to rise from around £5 billion in 2009-10 to around £14 billion in 2059-60.

C.16 The results were then combined with GDP projections (also at constant 2008-09 RPI prices) to show benefit payments as a proportion of GDP.

GDP projections

C.17 The Commission constructed GDP projections by using the 2008-09 outturn and GDP growth projections to 2015-16 as contained in the OBR forecast, these are detailed in Table C.3.

Table C.3: OBR forecasts for GDP growth

Forecast	2009-10	2010-11	2011-12	2012-13	2013-14	2014-15	2015-16
Real GDP growth (%)	-3.7	1.8	2.4	2.9	2.8	2.7	2.7

Source OBR

C.18 Beyond 2016-17, the Commission used GDP growth projections in line with the principal GDP growth projections in the December 2009 Long-term public finance report. The significant underlying assumptions for these projections are as follows:

- productivity growth of 2 per cent per annum;

- employment growth of 0.5 per cent per annum until 2048-49, and then 0.25 per cent from 2049-50 to 2059; and

- there is consistency in the long-term assumptions between benefit payments and GDP projections. For example, long-term real earnings growth is set equal to productivity growth in both sets of projections.

Historical benefit payments as a percentage of GDP

C.19 The Commission also calculated benefit payments as a percentage of GDP from 1999-2000 onwards to provide some historical context for the projections. These figures are also in constant 2008-09 RPI prices and were calculated using GDP figures from the Office of National Statistics and using benefit payments and employee contributions based on figures for the four largest unfunded schemes from the National Audit Office's March 2010 report on the cost of public service pensions.

Results

C.20 The resulting benefit payments, for all unfunded schemes, as a percentage of GDP are set out in the chart C.2:

Chart C.2: Projected benefit payments as a percentage of GDP – central projection

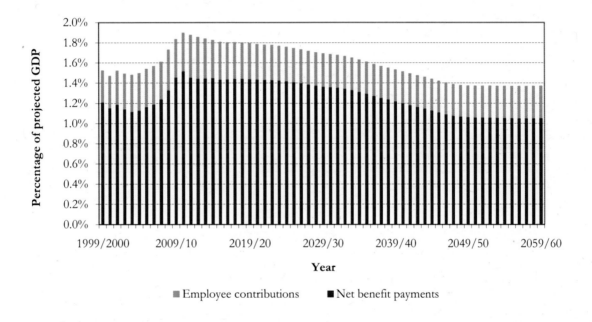

Source IPSPC calculation based on GAD, HM Treasury and OBR data.

C.21 In order to show the sensitivity of these calculations to the assumptions chosen, the Commission asked GAD to repeat its analysis using alternative assumptions, designed to be 'high cost' and 'low cost' scenarios once combined with consistent GDP projections. These assumptions are detailed in Table C.4.

Table C.4: Key long-term assumptions

Projection	Life expectancy (ONS 2008)	Real Earnings growth (%)	Public sector workforce growth (%)
Central	Principal life expectancy	2.00	0.25
'Low cost'	Low life expectancy	2.25	0.00
'High cost'	High life expectancy	1.75	0.50

Source: IPSPC

C.22 The GDP projections were also adjusted so that productivity assumptions are equal to real earnings growth. Lower real earnings growth is a high cost scenario as GDP projections reduce by more than benefit payment projections due to lower productivity growth.

C.23 The effect of changing these assumptions on benefit payments in constant RPI prices can be seen in the Chart C.3.

Chart C.3: Projected benefit payments at constant 2008-09 RPI prices

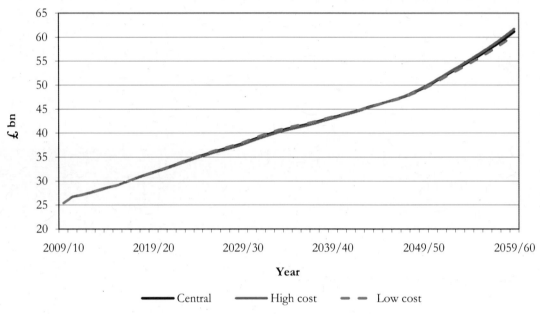

Source: GAD.

C.24 It can be seen that the effect of higher real earnings growth in the low cost scenario is more than offset by the lower life expectancy and public sector workforce growth. The reverse is true in the high cost scenario. Broadly, actual benefit payments vary little between the scenarios.

C.25 The main difference arises when equivalent assumptions are applied to the GDP projections in terms of productivity growth and longevity. This gives the results detailed in Chart C.4.

Chart C.4: Projected GDP at constant 2008-09 RPI prices

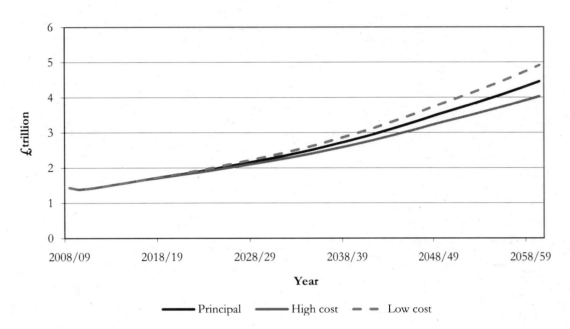

Source: IPSPC calculation based on GAD, HM Treasury and OBR data..

C.26 In the low cost scenario, GDP is significantly higher due to increased productivity and higher life expectancy leading to slightly larger employment growth. The reverse is true for the high cost scenario.

C.27 These projections were then combined to produce a fan chart showing a possible range of outcomes for benefit payments as a percentage of GDP, these are detailed in Chart C.5.

Chart C.5: Projected benefit payments as a percentage of GDP – sensitivity analysis

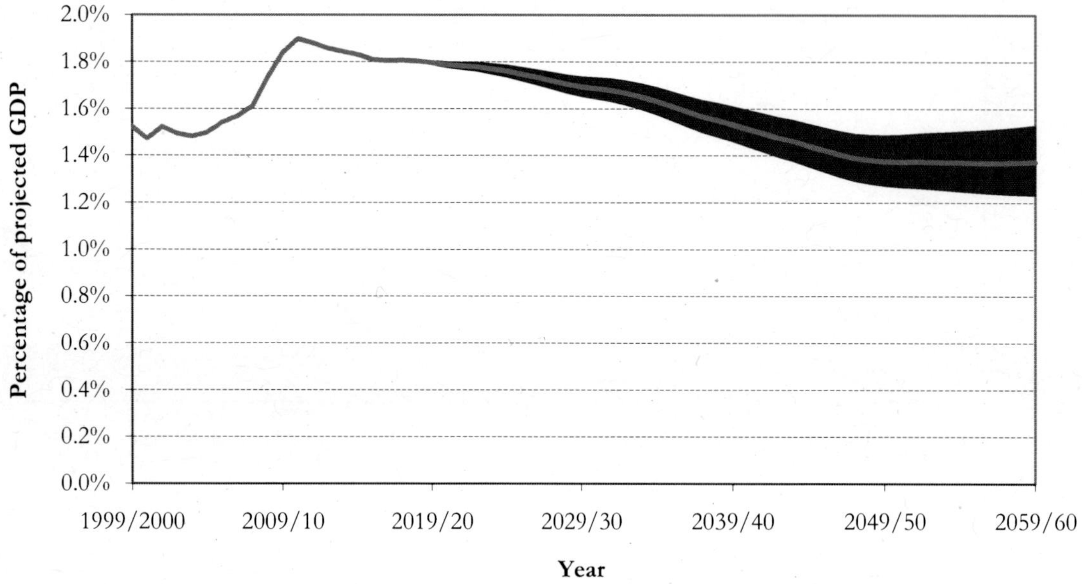

Source: IPSPC calculations based on GAD, HM Treasury and OBR data.

C.28 This sensitivity analysis does not show the full range of outcomes possible and it is conceivable that actual benefit payments as a percentage of GDP fall outside of this range. The sensitivity analysis does not investigate the implications of CPI diverging from RPI by more or less than 0.75 per cent. The Commission estimates that if the long-term gap was 0.5 per cent rather than 0.75 per cent, the projected costs could be higher by around a further 0.1 per cent of GDP.

Cap and share

C.29 As discussed above, both the Commission's and the December 2009 projections include allowance for the existing cap and share regime. Further details of the methodology used to apply cap and share can be found in Annex B of their 6 April 2010 methodology document, but broadly it is assumed that two thirds of cost pressures which fall to employees through cap and share will be met through benefit reductions, with the other third leading to employee contribution increases.

C.30 The effect of cap and share on the central projections of benefit payments and benefit payments as a percentage of GDP can be found in the Charts C.6 and C.7.

Chart C.6: Effect of cap and share – central projection

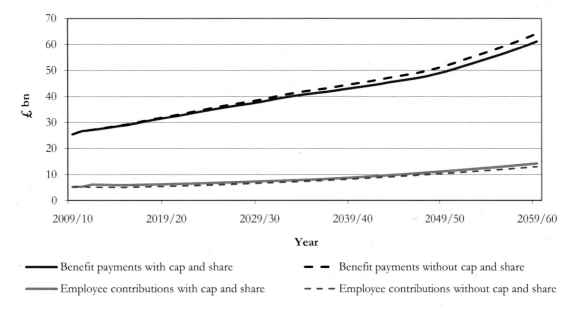

Source: GAD

Chart C.7: Projected benefit payments and employee contributions as a percentage of GDP

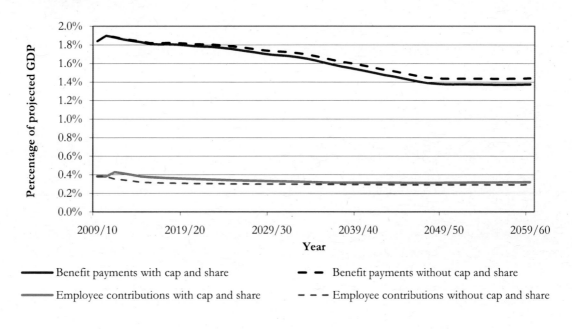

Source: IPSPC calculations based on GAD, HM Treasury and OBR data.

C.31 The allowance for cap and share assumes an increase in employee contributions in 2011-12 as a result of the ongoing actuarial valuations using life expectancy assumptions higher than those in previous valuations. This is also assumed to lead to lower benefit payments in the longer term. Overall the effect of cap and share on total benefit payments is just less than 0.1 per cent of GDP in 2059-60. However, it should be noted that the effect of cap and share is very sensitive to the assumptions adopted and future valuation outcomes and the impact in practice may be significantly more or less than this.

Split of benefit payments by membership

C.32 The Commission also asked GAD to split benefit payments by current type of membership for the central scenario. The results of this can be found in Chart C.8.

Chart C.8: Membership breakdown – central projection

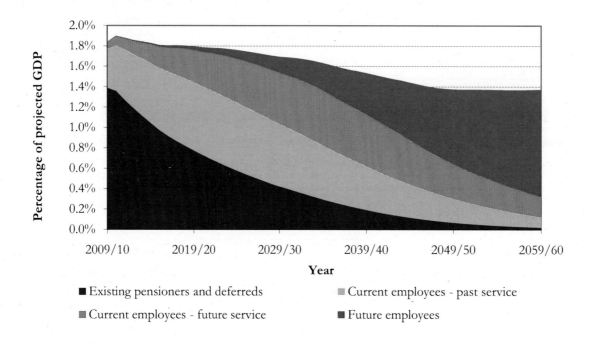

Source: IPSPC calculations based on GAD, HM Treasury and OBR data.

C.33 The significant amount of benefit payments for existing actives past service in the first year relate to tax-free cash lump sums on retirement. Those for existing actives future service reflect death benefits.

D Summary of evidence

D.1 On the 28 June, Lord Hutton, wrote an article in the Financial Times calling for all interested parties to contact the Commission directly with their comments and views on pensions reform. The Commission also wrote directly to interested groups in the first week of July to ask for evidence in assisting the Commission with its interim report. Lord Hutton received evidence from over 100 organisations and numerous individuals who had responded by the end of August with their contributions.

D.2 Stakeholder responses to the 'call for evidence' have tended to focus around five main issues.

The cost of pension provision now and in the future

D.3 First, a majority of respondents were concerned about the cost of pension provision at present and in the future. Most felt that public service pensions as they stand are unsustainable in the long-term. As a result, the majority of stakeholders have called for reform, although, some suggested that reform should wait until the completion of the comprehensive spending review. A second group, however, felt that the pensions liability was under control, noting that funded schemes like the LGPS do not contribute to the UK's structural deficit.

D.4 There was a significant amount of debate regarding the urgency and necessary magnitude of potential reforms. There was great variability in the valuation of pension costs and the measurements used. Accordingly, a number of commentators have called for updated figures and projections in advance of any recommendations.

D.5 Those who did call for cost savings felt that substantial reform – whether through scheme restructuring, a change in accrual rates, or an increase in the retirement age – would not produce results in the short-term. Most agree that the only driver of rapid savings will be an increase in employee contribution rates.

Recruitment and retention

D.6 Second, a large number of stakeholders placed a high value on public service pensions for the recruitment and retention of staff. Across a range of sectors, it was felt that good pensions were a necessary tool with which to compete with the private sector, especially against a background of economic recovery and accelerating private sector starting salaries.

High quality pensions were viewed by organisations not only as a tool to attract and retain staff, but to motivate them around the image of being a 'good employer'.

D.7 Specifically, respondents focused on the recruitment and retention of high-level staff that tend to be older and more experienced. In addition, older staff were seen as valuing pensions more highly than younger staff as part of the overall remuneration package.

D.8 The cost of turnover in organisations was also highlighted. Some suggested that higher turnover of skilled staff due to reformed public service pensions may nullify any potential savings from public service pension reform. There was debate over the time it would take for reforms to impact on recruitment and retention. Some felt that reform would have an immediate effect; others recognised the potential short-term gains, but warned of a long-term impact on attracting staff.

RPI to CPI

D.9 Third, concern was expressed over the change in indexation from RPI to CPI. Many argued that this switch would wipe a great deal off the value of their pensions and viewed it as a breach of the accrued rights of public service staff. Some felt that this apparent erosion of accrued rights could have a detrimental impact on a wider savings culture.

D.10 Though some respondents appreciated the financial rationale behind the initiative, most were not in favour.

Balance of pension provision between public and private sector

D.11 Fourth, a high number of respondents felt that the fundamental problem in pension provision lay in the erosion of high quality private service pensions. Accordingly, they often argued that an overall pensions strategy should be targeting adequate provision for all. Some viewed public service pensions as a benchmark for nation-wide adequacy and excellence, calling for retention of defined benefit pensions rather than a wholesale switch to defined contribution schemes. There was also a view that public service pensions are not 'gold-plated', and that an average public service salary is lower than its private sector equivalent.

D.12 A minority expressed concern over the long-term sustainability of the current balance between public and private sector pensions. It was seen as unfair that taxpayers funded public service pensions, whilst also tending to receive poorer provision than in the past in the private sector.

D.13 Many called for a more accurate system of comparative analysis between schemes and sectors. They felt that a lack of this was driving media concentration on a few 'outlier' cases. Some also criticised the public sector for contributing to a non-level playing field. The requirements to provide a 'broadly comparable' pension were in particular viewed as a barrier to the provision of competitive outsourcing.

Protection of accrued rights

D.14 Fifth, many stakeholders expressed concern over possible impacts on their accrued rights. There was also widespread confusion as to what exactly accrued rights meant. Some felt that it was reasonable to protect previously accrued benefits, but loosen restrictions around future accruals. Others saw an interference in future accruals for schemes already in place as unreasonable. Most asked for clarification around this issue.

Other points of interest

D.15 Responses to the call for evidence covered a range of other points. In particular:

- there are noticeable differentials in public service provision. Employer and employee contribution rates, for example, vary enormously from scheme to scheme. In addition, the nature of different professions – some bear more risk than others – is a factor in the adequacy of pension provision;

- the question of risk requires careful examination – not only between taxpayer and employee, but also between generations. It may not be fair that one generation tends to fund the pensions of a previous (or future) generation; and

- cost-savings will need to be examined strategically, with a view to the long-term as well as the impact on different sectors of society. In particular, the wider budget landscape will have to be considered, so that immediate savings in pensions do not lead to increased demand for means-tested benefits in the future.

Chart D.1: Number of stakeholders and the issues they raised

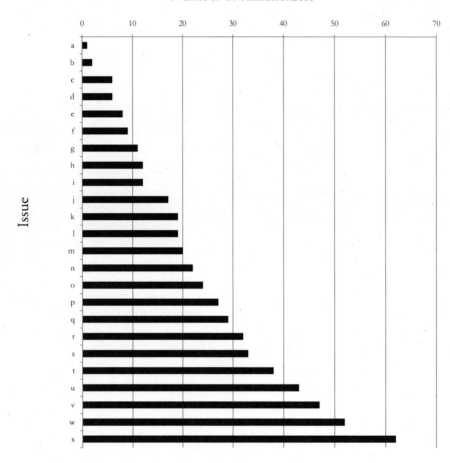

Source: Repsonses from 'Call of Evidence', July 2010.

Key

a Clarity over their legal framework and who holds responsibility

b Members understand any trade-offs

c Deal flexibly with specific job issues

d Understanding worth of benefits

e Easy to understand

f Practicality of implementation

g Clearly and transparently express costs to taxpayer

h Discount rate

i Regard to different professions

j Whole benefits and credits landscape

k Entire benefits package

l Overall remuneration package

m Support labour mobility

n Transitional arrangements

o Managing the risks of the pension provision to HMG and taxpayer

p Merits of funded and unfunded scheme structures

q Adequacy

r Distribution between public servants

s Protecting accrued rights

t Distribution of the costs of benefits between the employee and the taxpayer (and between generations)

u Balance of pension provision between private and public sector

v Baseline/recent reforms

w Recruitment and retention

x Public Sector Pensions cost at the moment and in the future

E Panel of Experts

As well as benefiting from the wide range of evidence received I have established a small group of academics and other experts, who have assisted me, mainly on a one-to-one basis, in shaping my views and have provided helpful comments on this report. I am grateful to them all for their help, however the report represents my views alone.

The panel members are:

- Ron Amy OBE;

- Professor Nicholas Barr;

- Lord Bichard[1] of Nailsworth;

- Professor David Blake;

- Niki Cleal;

- Baroness Jeannie Drake CBE;

- Carl Emmerson;

- Professor John Hills; and

- Professor Alasdair Smith.

1 Lord Bichard will be advising the Commission for the second half of the review.

F List of charts and tables

Charts

Tables

 **Glossary**

Accrual: A payment earned in one period but not paid until a later period.

Active Members: These are current employees who are contributing (or have contributions made on their behalf) to an organisation's occupational pension scheme. They are distinct from deferred members and pensioners.

Accrual rate: The proportion of earnings that a defined benefit (DB) pension scheme pays as pension for each year of membership. For example, a scheme with an accrual rate of 1/60 provides 1/60th of earnings for each year of membership, which is higher than a pension based on an accrual rate of 1/80 of earnings.

Accrued Liabilities: A measure of the value, in today's money, of all pension entitlements to be paid in the future that have been earned to date.

Accrued Rights: Rights to pension and other benefits under scheme rules, deriving directly or indirectly from membership of the scheme. Such rights include pension awards already received and pensionable service built up so far based on a particular pension age. However, there is no standard definition of accrued rights across public service pension schemes: the rights will depend on specific circumstances, such as the terms of the individual pension schemes.

Actuarial valuation: A report of the financial position of a DB pension scheme carried out by an actuary every three or four years. The report typically sets out the scheme's assets and liabilities as at the date of the valuation; the rate at which the sponsoring employer must contribute to meet the liabilities accruing as they become due; and the additional rate at which the employer must contribute to eradicate any deficit (the excess of liabilities over assets) within a stated time period.

Additional Benefits: These are benefits in addition to the pension under a scheme that Active Members may purchase to add to the pension ("added pension"), the years of pensionable service ("added years"), or for a separate money purchase pension ("additional voluntary contributions").

Additional Voluntary Contribution (AVC): These are personal pension contributions made by someone who is also a member of an occupational scheme as a top-up to their occupational entitlement. AVCs can be made into the occupational scheme or to a stand-alone product called a Freestanding AVC plan.

Admitted Body Status: Admitted body status refers to the practice of the Local Government Pension Scheme of accepting as members the employees of bodies not covered by the original or primary ambit of the scheme as set out in its founding statute. It enables contractors, who take on an authority's services or functions with employees transferring from the authority, to offer the transferring staff continued eligibility of the transferring authority's pension scheme.

Annuity: A series of regular payments usually payable for the life of the annuitant. Annuities are usually purchased by a lump sum of cash. Pension schemes sometimes discharge their promise of pension benefit by purchasing an annuity. Individuals can purchase an annuity using their own capital. There is a wide range of options available e.g. level, escalating, guaranteed, single or joint lives.

Automatic enrolment: A pension scheme where an individual is made a member by default and has actively to decide to leave the scheme.

basic State Pension (bSP): Non-earnings-related pension based on an individual's National Insurance Contribution record.

Cap and Share: This is an arrangement applying to the pension schemes for the NHS, Teachers, Civil Service and Local Government, whereby increases or reductions in the costs of a scheme identified in a pension scheme actuarial valuation are shared between employees and employers up to the value of the cap. Above the cap the increases or reductions are borne by employees, either by changing employee contributions or the cost of employee benefits or both. Below the cap, increases or reductions are shared between employers and employees.

Capped DB scheme: A DB pension scheme where a limit is placed on pension entitlement, for example by placing a ceiling on the amount of annual earnings that are pensionable or by limiting the amount of pension that might be awarded under scheme rules.

Career Average Scheme: A defined benefit scheme that gives individuals a pension based on a percentage of the salary earned in each year of their working life.

Cash balance scheme: A scheme where the employer puts a notional amount into the member's pension pot every year, which is then guaranteed. This credit can be expressed as a percentage of salary for each year worked. If cash contributions from the employee and employer, plus investment returns, do not match this promised "notional credit" then the employer has to meet any shortfall. On retirement the resulting "cash balance" can be used to purchase an annuity or to make other arrangements for retirement.

CETV (Cash Equivalent Transfer Value): The value of accrued pension rights when any worker ceases to be an active member of a scheme before pension is payable. Everyone can request a CETV except in the year before retirement but schemes can refuse to accept them.

Cohort Life Expectancy: The estimate of an individual's probability of surviving future years allowing for possible changes in mortality rates over time.

Collective DC scheme: All member pension contributions are placed in one fund that is then managed on behalf of the members. As in standard DC schemes the pensions will vary according to the value of the underlying investments. However, within collective DC schemes there is the option to spread the effects across the various groups of members ("intergenerational sharing") to smooth the effects of market conditions.

Combination hybrid scheme: Where members simultaneously earn benefits that are part DB and DC.

Commission: The Independent Public Service Pensions Commission.

Commutation factor: A number used to convert a pension annuity into a lump sum. The factor usually depends on the sex of the member and the age at which the conversion takes place. The factors are scheme specific and are either set out in the pension scheme's rules or are updated periodically by the scheme's trustees or administrators.

Conditional Indexation: Where the uprating of a pension fund or pensions in payment each year is variable and dependent on other factors, such as investment returns.

Consumer Prices Index (CPI): It is an internationally comparable measure of inflation based on structures in international legislation and guidelines and launched in 1996. Like the Retail Prices Index (RPI) it tracks the changing cost of a fixed basket of goods and services over time. However unlike the RPI it disregards some items, such as housing costs. It also has a different population base for the indices from the RPI and a different way in which the index is calculated.

Cost Sharing: The cost of any benefit increases is shared between individual and employer.

Contracting-out: The facility to opt out of the additional state pension and build up benefits in a private pension scheme.

Current contribution rate: The standard contribution rate as adjusted for past surpluses and deficits and payable by employers and employees

Current Service Cost: A measure of the value of the new pension promises built up over a year.

Death Benefit Lump Sum: See Death in service.

Death in retirement benefit: A pension scheme benefit that is usually paid to the spouse of a scheme member if that member dies after retirement. The benefit typically takes the form of a pension paid to the dependant of a proportion of the pension the member was receiving when he or she died.

Death In Service benefit: A pension scheme benefit which is usually paid to the spouse (or sometimes other nominated dependant) of a scheme member if that member dies whilst an active member. The benefit typically takes the form of a lump sum (Death Benefit Lump Sum), calculated as a multiple of salary, plus a pension paid to the dependant of a proportion of the pension the member would have received if he or she had lived until retirement age.

Deferred Members: Deferred members are scheme members who have left employment, or ceased to be an active member of the scheme whilst remaining in employment, but retain an entitlement to a pension from the scheme.

Defined Benefit (DB) Pension Scheme: A pension scheme where the pension is related to the members' salary or some other value fixed in advance.

Defined Contribution (DC) Pension Scheme: A scheme where the individual receives a pension based on the contributions made and the investment return that they have produced. These are sometimes referred to as money purchase schemes.

Deferred Pension Benefit: The benefit awarded to a defined benefit scheme member who has left the scheme.

Dependent Member: An individual who is eligible to receive retirement benefits following the death of a scheme member.

Employee Contribution Rates: The percentage of their pensionable salary that employees pay as a contribution towards a pension.

Employer Contribution Rates: The percentage of the salary of employees that employers pay as a contribution towards the employees' pension.

Employer Covenant: The willingness and ability of an employer to support the pension scheme in the long-term.

Fair Deal: A non-statutory code of practice introduced in 1999 that protects the pension provisions of public sector workers that have their employment compulsorily transferred out of the public sector. In such a situation the transferring organisation is required to ensure that the pension provision for future service is "broadly comparable" after the transfer.

Final salary scheme: A DB scheme that gives individuals a pension based on the number of years of pensionable service, the accrual rate and final earnings as defined by the scheme.

FRS17: A financial reporting standard that sets out accounting treatment for retirement benefits.

Funded: Pension schemes in which pension contributions are paid into a fund that is invested and pensions are paid out of this pot.

IAS19: An international accounting standard that sets out the accounting treatment for employee benefits, including post-employment benefits such as pensions.

Index Linked Gilt Yields: Gilts are UK government bonds, the benchmarks for the sterling fixed income markets. Yields shown for index-linked gilts are based on an assumed inflation rate.

Indexation: The technique used to adjust income payments or the uprating of a pension fund in line with an index.

Interest Cost: Estimates the amount by which the value of accrued liabilities increased over a year as a result of the 'unwinding' of the discount rate, reflecting the fact that pension payments are closer to being paid.

Life expectancy: Life expectancy at a given age, x, is the average number of years that a male or female aged x will live thereafter.

Longevity: The length or duration of human life.

Maturity: The maturity of a pension scheme indicates the number of active members relative to the number of members receiving pensions. An immature scheme, such as the NHS scheme, is one that has more active members building up pensions than pensioner members receiving pensions.

Member contributions: The amounts paid by active scheme members into their pension schemes.

Mutualisation: Employee participation in, and of, an organisation. Implied sharing of the risks and benefits.

National Insurance (NI): The national system of benefits paid in specific situations, such as retirement, based on compulsory earnings-related contributions by employers and employees. Self-employed people make contributions on a different basis.

NEST (National Employment Savings Trust): The arms length from Government, low cost pensions scheme associated with the automatic enrolment reforms planned for 2012.

Net Cash Expenditure: Benefits paid to recipients less contributions received by central government from employees and employers in one year.

Normal Pension age: The earliest age at which, in the normal course of events, a scheme member may retire with payment of his or her unreduced accrued superannuation benefits.

Normal Retirement Age: The age at which the employer is entitled to terminate the contract of employment on grounds of age. Age discrimination legislation presently prohibits this being less than 65 save in exceptional circumstances.

Notional Defined Contribution scheme: A scheme whereby the values of the pensions at retirement are determined by an assumed return on contributions and an annuity rate or rates.

Normal Retirement Age (NRA): The normal retirement age (NRA) is the age at which retirement benefits (before rounding) are equal to the "primary insurance amount."

Occupational Pension: A pension, which is provided via the employer, but from a pension scheme that takes the form of a trust arrangement and is legally separate from the employer.

Old-age dependency ratio: The number of people above 65 to the number of people aged 18 or 20 to 64 in the population.

Pay As You Go (PAYG): See "Unfunded Pension Schemes."

Pensioner Member: Individuals who now draw a pension and who are mainly former employees. However they may also include widows, widowers and other dependants of former active members.

Independent Public Service Pensions Commission: An independent commission undertaking a fundamental structural review of public service pension provision by Budget 2011

Pension credit: The main income-related benefit for pensioners, which combines the Guarantee Credit and the Savings Credit.

Pension replacement ratio: Income in retirement as a proportion of income before retirement.

Period Life Expectancy: Represents the amount of time an individual is expected to live if mortality rates were equal to the experience of other individuals in that year.

Public sector pension schemes: These comprise both public service pension schemes and other schemes in the wider public sector such as the BBC, Transport for London, the Bank of England and the Royal Mail. These schemes are not authorised by statute and the organisation concerned makes the rules of the schemes.

Public Sector Transfer Club: A group of some 120 salary related occupational pension schemes. It allows easier movement of staff mainly within the public sector. It does this by making sure that employees receive broadly equivalent credits when they transfer their pensionable service to their new scheme regardless of any increase in salary when they move to their new employment.

Public service pension schemes: Pension schemes authorised by statute where the relevant Ministers make the rules of the schemes. The main schemes are those for civil servants, the armed forces, NHS employees, teachers, local government employees, the police and firefighters. There are over 200 public service pension schemes.

Public Services Forum (PSF) Agreement: An agreement in October 2005 between trades unions and the then Government, made at the Public Services Forum run by the Government, on how reforms to public service pension schemes should be taken forward.

Retail Prices Index (RPI): It is a measure of inflation and like the Consumer Prices Index (CPI) it tracks the changing cost of a fixed basket of goods and services over time. However, unlike the CPI it takes into account items such as housing costs. It also has a different population base for the indices from the CPI and a different way in which the index is calculated.

SCAPE (Superannuation Contributions Adjusted for Past Experience): A methodology used to set employer contribution rates across public service intended to mirror the operation of a funded scheme by keeping track of a notional 'Pension Account'.

Scheme liabilities: The scheme liabilities at a given date are an estimate of the total value of future payments that the scheme will have to make to all scheme members in respect of pension rights which have been earned before that date.

Sequential hybrid scheme: A pension scheme where a member may earn both a DB pension and a DC pension during their career with an employer. Members earn either a DB or DC benefit at any one time.

Social Time Preference: The value society places on current consumption as opposed to future consumption.

Standard Contribution Rate: The total rate of contributions (employer plus employee) which would need to be paid in order to meet the cost of pension benefits accruing over a defined period, expressed as a percentage of payroll.

State Earnings Related Pension Schemes (SERPS): The forerunner of the State Second Pension, which provides an earnings-related National Insurance pension based on contributions.

State Pension Age (SPA): The age at which an individual can claim their state pension. It is currently 65 for men and 60 for women. The SPA for women will gradually increase to 65 between 2010 and 2020.

State Second Pension (S2P): The National Insurance pension that gives benefits based on an individual's earnings and contributions.

Top-up DC: Where a DC arrangement is available to supplement another form of pension provided by an employer.

TUPE: Transfer of Undertakings (Protection of Employment) Regulations 2006.

Unfunded Pension Schemes: Pension schemes, which are not backed by a pension fund. Instead current contributions are used to pay current pensions along with other funds provided by the employer. Most public service schemes are unfunded, except for the Local Government scheme, which is funded.

H Abbreviations

AFCS	Armed Forces Compensation Scheme
AFPS	Armed Forces Pension Scheme
bSP	Basic State Pension
CARE	Career Average Revalued Earnings
CETV	Cash Equivalent Transfer Value
CIPFA	Chartered Institute of Public Finance and Accounting
CPI	Consumer Price Index
DB	Defined Benefit
DC	Defined Contribution
DCLG	Department of Communities and Local Government
DDA	Disability Discrimination Act
DWP	Department for Work and Pensions
ECHR	European Court of Human Rights
FPS	Firefighters' Pension Scheme
GAD	Government Actuary's Department
GDP	Gross Domestic Product
ILO	International Labour Organisation
IFS	Institute for Fiscal Studies
IPSPC	Independent Public Service Pensions Commission
LA	Local Authority
LFS	Labour Force Survey
LGPS	Local Government Pension Scheme
LTPFR	Long-Term Public Finance Report
NAO	National Audit Office
NEST	National Employment Savings Trust
NFPS	New Firefighters' Pension Scheme
NHS	National Health Service
NPA	Normal Pension Age
NRA	Normal Retirement Age
OBR	Office for Budget Responsibility

OECD	Organisation for Economic Co-operation and Development
ONS	Office for National Statistics
OPSS	Occupational Pension Scheme Survey
PAYG	Pay As You Go
PBR	Pre-Budget Report
PCSPS	Principle Civil Service Pension Scheme
PESA	Public Expenditure Statistical Analysis
PPI	Pensions Policy Institute
PRB	Pay Review Body
PSF	Public Service Forum
PSPC	Public Sector Pay Committee
PSPS	Public Service Pensions Schemes
RPI	Retail Price Index
SERPS	State Earnings Related Pension Schemes
SSP/S2P	State Second Pension
SPA	State Pension Age
TPS	Teachers' Pension Scheme
TUPE	Transfer of Undertakings Protection of Employment
UKAEA	UK Atomic Energy Authority
USS	Universities Superannuation Scheme

Bibliography

Audit Commission (2010), *Local government pensions in England: An information paper*

Barrell, R. and Weale, M. (2010), *'Fiscal policy, fairness between generations and national saving'*, Oxford Review of Economic Policy, Vol. 26, No. 1, pp. 87-116

Cabinet Office (2000), *Staff Transfers in the Public Sector: Statement of Practice*

Cabinet Office (2010), *Draft Structural Reform Plan*

Clery, E., McKay, S., Phillips, M. and Robinson, C. (2007), *'Attitudes to pensions: the 2006 survey'*, Department for Work and Pensions Research Report No. 434

Crawford, R., Emmerson, C. and Tetlow, G. (2010), *'Occupational Pension Value in the Public and Private Sectors'*, IFS Working Paper W10/03

Department for Communities and Local Government (2010), *Local Government Financial Statistics England*, No. 20

Disney, R., Emmerson, C. and Tetlow, G. (2007), *'Pension Rights, Choice of Pension Plan and Job Mobility in Britain'*, mimeo

Disney, R., Emmerson, C. and Tetlow, G. (2009), *'What is a Public Sector Pension Worth?'*, Economic Journal, Vol. 119, Issue 541, pp. F517-F535

Disney, R. and Gosling, A. (2008), *'Changing Public Sector Wage Differentials in the UK'*, IFS Working Paper WP08/02

Gilling-Smith, G.D. (1968), *The Complete Guide to Pensions and Superannuation*, Penguin

Government Actuary's Department (2010), *Pay-As-You-Go Public Service Pension Schemes December 2009 Cashflow Projections: Methodology, data and assumptions*

HM Government (2010), *The Coalition: Our programme for government*

HM Treasury (2003), *The Green Book: Appraisal and Evaluation in Central Government*

HM Treasury (2009), *Long-term public finance report: an analysis of fiscal sustainability*

HM Treasury (2009), *Pre-Budget Report 2009*, Cm 7747

HM Treasury (2010), *Public Expenditure Statistical Analyses 2010*

Howse, K. (2007), *'Updating the debate on intergenerational fairness in pension reform'*, Oxford Institute of Ageing Working Paper 107

Hymans Robertson (2009), *Public Sector Pensions – A Frontline Perspective*

Institute for Fiscal Studies (2008), *The IFS Green Budget January 2008*

Institute for Fiscal Studies (2010), *The IFS Green Budget February 2010*

Levy, S., Mitchell, H., Guled, G. and Coleman, J. (2010), *'Total reward: pay and pension contributions in the private and public sectors'*, Economic and Labour Market Review, Vol. 4, No. 9

National Audit Office (2010), *The Cost of Public Service Pensions*

Office for Budget Responsibility (2010), *Pre-budget forecast June 2010*

Office for Budget Responsibility (2010), *Budget forecast June 2010*

Office for Budget Responsibility (2010), *Budget 2010: The Economy & Public Finances – supplementary material*

Office for National Statistics (2009), *Occupational Pension Schemes Annual Report 2008*

Palacios, R. and Whitehouse, E. (2006), *'Civil Service Pension Schemes around the World'*, World Bank Social Protection Discussion Paper No. 0602

Pensions Commission (2004), *Pensions: Challenges and Choices – The First Report of the Pensions Commission*

Pensions Commission (2005), *A New Pension Settlement for the Twenty-First Century - The Second Report of the Pensions Commission*

Pensions Policy Institute (2008), *An assessment of the Government's reforms to public sector pensions*

Pensions Policy Institute (2010), *Public sector pension schemes: policy objectives and options for the future*

The Pensions Regulator (2009), *Scheme funding: An analysis of recovery plans*

Review Body on Senior Salaries (2010), *Thirty-Second Report on Senior Salaries*, Cm 7804

Shaw, C. (2007), *'Fifty years of United Kingdom national population projections: how accurate have they been?'*, Population Trends, No. 128, Office for National Statistics

Stern, N. (2007), *The Economics of Climate Change: The Stern Review*, Cambridge University Press

Sutcliffe, C. (2007), *'Should Defined Benefit Pension Schemes be Career Average or Final Salary'*, ICMA Centre Discussion Papers in Finance, DP 2007-6